Seeds of the Seventies

Seeds of the Seventies

Values, Work, and Commitment in Post-Vietnam America

Arthur Stein

Published for University of Rhode Island
by University Press of New England
Hanover and London, 1985

For Mom and Dad,
and Lisa and Jody

University Press of New England

Brandeis University

Brown University

Clark University

University of Connecticut

Dartmouth College

University of New Hampshire

University of Rhode Island

Tufts University

University of Vermont

Printed in the United States of America

LIBRARY OF CONGRESS CATALOGING IN PUBLICATION DATA

Stein, Arthur Benjamin.
    Seeds of the seventies.

    Bibliography: p.
    Includes index.
    1. United States—Social conditions—1970–
2. Social values.   I. University of Rhode Island.
II. Title.
HN 59.S743   1985   306'.0973   84-40597
ISBN 0-87451-332-4
ISBN 0-87451-343-X (pbk.)

Contents

Seeds of the Seventies

Introduction

In the 1980s the United States is struggling to develop a renewed sense of purpose and direction. Despite material abundance the nation is beset with an all-too-familiar agenda of problems to resolve, both at home and abroad. Indeed, America's great but sometimes unfulfilled potential tends to magnify the frustrations a substantial number of its citizens feel.

What is our legacy from the immediate past? Broadly speaking, the early 1960s are remembered as years of social ferment, a time when youthful idealism found an outlet in the newly formed Peace Corps and in the civil rights movement. Then came the Vietnam War, culturally disruptive but marked by considerable political activism.

In contrast, Tom Wolfe and other critics have dubbed the 1970s the "Me Decade"—a time of extreme individualism and pursuit of narrowly defined self-interest. (This negative characterization could be extended to the early 80s as well.)

Perhaps the best of the literature on the social pathology of the time is Christopher Lasch's *The Culture of Narcissism,* which describes "a way of life that is dying—the culture of competitive individualism, which in its decadence has carried . . . the pursuit of happiness to the dead end of a narcissistic preoccupation with the self."[1]

One can appreciate the pungency of these critiques and share their deep concerns, but the prospect of a society with little hope for change or redemption is a bleak one and does not fully take into consideration the enduring and positive qualities of the many-faceted American experience.

In deciding to research and write this book, I felt the necessity to identify some of the more promising alternatives and portents of positive change already present or being developed within America. As the book evolved it came to center on, although it is not confined to, the 1970s.

The rapid changes and social upheavals of the Vietnam years were disorienting to many lives. For example, some of those directly involved in antiwar activity had to restabilize their personal lives in the aftermath of the conflict. Looking for new directions, some turned to the "human potential" movement, others began to explore various spiritually oriented traditions, while yet others channeled their energies into projects for social and political change in their own communities.

This time of reassessment has received surprisingly little attention from cultural commentators and scholars. A basic purpose of this study, therefore, is to give a sense of what was happening beneath the surface in the 1970s rather than to emphasize the more visible excesses, the trendy, and the bizarre.

What emerges is a wide diversity of individuals, groups, and movements actively engaged in innovative socially and politically concerned activities. Many of these people and organizations speak of social justice and a more peaceful world order. Some seek to build alternative institutional forms, while others work at a variety of traditional occupations within existing societal structures. Some say they are primarily engaged in "working on themselves" and becoming more "centered," in the belief that a person can best be a social reformer by first re-forming himself or herself. Most would not want to be placed in any one category. They do not belong to a common movement as such. They do, though, share an aspiration to build more integrated lives for themselves and to contribute to positive developments in their communities.

A broad cross section of "new alternatives" people includes, among others, individuals who are involved with participatory politics, women's and minority rights, concerns of children and senior citizens, producer and consumer cooperatives, peace conversion economics, worker-owned businesses, neighborhood redevelopment, protection of the environment, revitalization of traditional religious structures, and communities moving toward more self-sufficiency. Also, there are groups and demonstration centers working on appropriate technologies, alternative energy sources, holistic health care, organic farming, and skills exchange.

A substantial majority of those involved in such activities hold the basic premise that many of our nation's problems are rooted in present societal imbalances caused by overspecialization, extreme competitiveness, wastefulness, and alienation. Those who seek constructive changes are attempting to emphasize alternative values, such as cooperation, more simple living, eco-community, and recognition of the interdependence of all life-forms.

At least seven fundamental ideas or affirmative values characterize the alternatives movement at its best. Together they constitute an antithesis to the "Me-Decade" stereotype. They include

1. A willingness, and a desire, to become more self-reliant and less dependent on "the system"

2. An inclusiveness rather than exclusiveness in dealing with people and ideas, and a commitment to the pursuit of social justice

3. A movement toward human-scaled institutions and new, more cooperative forms of community

4. An emphasis on quality of life, including care for the natural environment and all life-forms

5. Reference to a principled ethos or set of values as a guide for daily living

6. A quest for greater self-understanding, to become more centered

7. A movement toward voluntarily simplifying one's life-style and applying the principle of nonviolence to one's social philosophy

In various parts of the country today a significant minority of people identify with many of these values and are seeking to integrate them wherever possible into their lives. The pathway has not always been clear. There were false starts and there was (and still is) much serious questioning, for personal and communitarian growth does not come ready-made. Accomplishments have been accompanied by setbacks. These professed ideals and values are not easy to live up to. But as a result of sustained effort, fresh insights and renewed purposefulness are emerging.

In an age that has produced horrors such as Auschwitz, the Gulags, and Hiroshima, the human capacity for destructive behavior is obvious. However, the constructive side of the picture also needs to be put forward—people who are having life-affirming experiences that may be useful to others in the broader society.

The subject of this book suggests both an aspiration and a challenge—to find ways to live and work together with mutual respect and understanding. The goal of community includes recognition of the needs of each individual, and also of the shared need to identify and build on interests that are held in common.

Focus on those identified with alternative and social change movements is in no way meant to diminish the valued contributions of those with equally humane concerns from every walk of life. There are people working for societal betterment in virtually every vocation, who, with little or no fanfare, are committed to activities that involve the welfare of others. Each person's input is significant in the journey toward finding that often elusive common ground.[2]

Some people and groups do not wear any special label. Yet their innovative endeavors can contribute significantly to the process of reorienting America. Some have worked for positive societal change for many years; the involvements of others are of more recent vintage. I am not so much concerned with ascertaining what is old or new under the sun, but what may be of value in our quest as a people to find renewed direction and purpose.

In a broad sense my inquiry draws on the tradition of human dignity and independent thought—the *real* American dream—

from Roger Williams and Thomas Jefferson to Abraham Lincoln and Eleanor Roosevelt. It harks back to the spirit of Dr. Martin Luther King, Jr., and to the ongoing struggles for a more just and caring society.

This story is basically about Americans and the land in which we live, our home and workplace. I join those who deplore expressions of American chauvinism. Yet this nation, which has the megapower to precipitate the destruction of humankind, also has great potential for doing good and exerting positive leadership. Virtually all the world's racial, religious, ethnic, and cultural traditions are found somewhere in America. In this sense the United States is a microcosm of the world's people, and all have an interest in the success of the American democratic experiment.

The current search for renewed direction transcends national boundaries. Fresh approaches drawing on the creative potential of the entire human family are required.

Every nation, and indeed each person, has a unique role to play in response to the life-threatening challenges of our age—not only to survive, but to develop a planetary consciousness more worthy of the name *homo sapiens*. In this context what happens here in the United States has major repercussions throughout the world.

Kingston, Rhode Island
October 1984

Notes

1. Christopher Lasch, *The Culture of Narcissism: American Life in an Age of Diminishing Expectations* (New York: Warner Books, 1980), p. xxv.
2. The thought of creating common ground is appearing in many areas: The Paul Winter Consort recording "Common Ground" celebrates the creatures of the wild, which have become endangered species. (In its disregard for other life-forms, humankind itself has become an endangered species.) A cooperative restaurant in Brattleboro, Vermont, called Common Ground provides nourishing food and fellowship. In

the San Francisco Bay Area, *Common Ground: Resources for Personal Transformation* circulates as a free directory of local resources. The Search for Common Ground, started in Washington, D.C., in 1983, brings together people from all points of the political spectrum—to better understand one another's points of view. And the list is growing.

Chapter 1

A Time for Reorientation:
An Overview of the 1970s

In the United States the early 1960s saw an outpouring of public involvement in various social and political causes. A reservoir of untapped youthful idealism led to the formation of the Peace Corps and the Students for a Democratic Society. People of all ages were inspired by the heroic nonviolent struggles of the civil rights campaigns led by Dr. Martin Luther King, Jr. The charismatic leadership of John and Robert Kennedy generated for many a sense of hope and meaningfulness in political participation.

The tragic deaths of these leaders unleashed much frustration and disillusionment. Meanwhile, the brief springtime of the "flower children" ended in the overrunning of San Francisco's Haight-Ashbury by a torrent of runaway teenagers, gawking tourists, and hard drugs. And the seemingly interminable war in Vietnam dragged on.

When direct American involvement in the Vietnam War finally ended, a number of the groups that had formed the antiwar movement went their separate ways, each promoting its own special interests or causes, or withdrawing from political activity altogether. Life for many did not return to "normal," though. Some of those whose lives had been profoundly affected by the events of the 1960s felt the need to develop a new orientation, to bring their lives back into balance. They felt that a time for reflection and reassessment was necessary. The subsequent search for renewed direction brought insight and many positive experiences, along with growing pains and excesses.[1]

A Variety of Paths

Critics have charged that the "consciousness movement" has given birth to a generation of narcissistic individuals. Indeed for many there has been too much emphasis on the narrowly defined self, to the exclusion of concern for the well-being of others. But this is not characteristic of most of those involved in the kind of reflective work on oneself that I will discuss.

Rather than self-obsession, emphasis is placed on self-reliance and taking more responsibility for one's own life and actions. This thread of individual independence extends historically from Jefferson through Thoreau to such present-day role models as Helen and Scott Nearing. An example is the movement toward owner-built homes—in the 1970s schools such as Heartwood in western Massachusetts and Cornerstones in Brunswick, Maine, were founded to teach the skills of house building, renovation, and maintenance.

Although the terms may sound similar, there is a great deal of difference between this concept of self-reliance and the ideas and policies of the Radical Right. Self-reliance and individual responsibility do not mean that governmental institutions should avoid their obligations to millions of people who do not have the education, health, or mental capacity to "make it on their own" in today's world. These people, along with those who cannot find employment during hard economic times, need and deserve the assistance of the broader society. Indeed, one of the truest indicators of a "good society" is how it treats those who lack the means to help themselves. But over the long run, many people and organizations involved with social change prefer programs of self-help and community cooperation rather than governmental subsidies, which foster dependence. The old saying "Give a man a fish and you feed him for a day, but teach him to fish and you feed him for a lifetime" is indicative of this approach. It is appropriate that an organization like Oxfam, whose philosophy and work embody helping others to uplift themselves, should have adopted this saying as its *logos*.

An emphasis on personal growth can often be combined with social and political involvement. Evidence of this link is found, for example, in the work of Mark Satin, who in 1979 helped establish the New World Alliance, a coalition that sought to bring together the more positive aspects of the left, right, and center of the American political spectrum. The formation of the Citizens Party in 1979–80 also indicated a renewed search for vehicles for political expression. The latter part of the 1970s was further marked by the development of increasingly broad-based movements against nuclear weapons and nuclear power plants.

This political rethinking suggests the quest for a new balance between the individual and society, going well beyond unbridled capitalism. However, it does not advocate either centralized state control as manifested under Marxist regimes or paternalistic "big government." Instead, it points to the need to develop middle ways between rampant individualism and extreme collectivism, and emphasizes the participatory nature of democracy.

Within the professional organizations of many of the natural and social sciences, reform-minded groups that recognize the need for enlivening changes have come into being. Groups such as the Union of Concerned Scientists, Physicians for Social Responsibility, the Caucus for a New Political Science, the Union of Radical Political Economists, and the Committee of Concerned Asian Scholars all evince a concern for the social and political implications of the work done by their respective professions.

A key word of the late 1960s was *counterculture,* referring to a rather amorphous movement in opposition to the dominant culture. By the mid-1970s, however, *alternative* had become a significant term. Developing alternatives to existing institutions and values was emphasized rather than merely being against those which one did not like. Middle America was left out of the counterculture; the gulf between the mainstream and the counterculture was vast in the society at large and even within many families. For the alternative culture length of hair and mode of dress are no longer as symbolically important as they were for both mainstream society and counterculture groups.

Interest in building integral health-care centers, food and housing cooperatives, learning centers, peer counseling programs, and the like was renewed in the 1970s. A wide range of groups, whose activities were often reported in magazines such as *The East-West Journal, Communities, Whole Life Times, New Age Journal,* and *New Roots* and in the useful publication *A Guide to Cooperative Alternatives,*[2] sprang up across the country. Rather than waiting for "the Revolution" to occur, people sought to establish parallel programs or institutions.

Most of the 1960s-style communes and attempts at building community unraveled after a few months or years. The 1970s, however, saw the maturation of several intentional communities begun in the late 1960s, among them Twin Oaks in Virginia, Ananda Cooperative Community in California, and The Farm in Tennessee. Contacts were also established with "New Age" communities overseas, like Findhorn in Scotland. The early 1980s saw groups such as the Sirius educational community near Amherst, Massachusetts, come into being.

Political and Economic Initiatives

Overall, the 1960s and 1970s were marked by a democratization of American life. Considerable gains were achieved in equality and social justice for blacks, women, gays, the handicapped, and the elderly. Society has become on the whole less rigid and overtly discriminatory.[3] Yet, from the vantage point of the previously excluded, the process has often been slow and not without painful setbacks. Much remains to be done.

In the civil rights movement the Reverend Ralph Abernathy has continued steadfastly as Dr. King's successor in the Southern Christian Leadership Conference. Some of the young southern blacks who participated in the freedom marches of the 1960s turned their attention to working for change within the political system. For example, Andrew Young was appointed ambassador to the United Nations for part of the Carter Administration and is currently the mayor of Atlanta. Julian Bond has served effectively for a number of terms in the Georgia state legislature. The Reverend Jesse Jackson organized Operation PUSH (People United for Self Help) in Chicago and then formed the Rainbow Coalition.

By the late 1970s many of the pop revolutionary figures of the Vietnam era had faded from the scene. But others conscientiously concerned with social justice and also well-known to the public at that time, are still involved in various capacities. For example, Dave Dellenger continues his broad-based work within the peace community. Tom Hayden has become an innovative state legislator in California. Brothers Philip and Daniel Berrigan and Daniel Ellsberg are committed to the eventual dismantling of the nuclear arsenal and have put themselves on the line in actions involving nonviolent civil disobedience.

This list is noticeably devoid of women, not because women did not make vital contributions to the civil rights and antiwar movements, but because—except for a few, like Bella Abzug (who opposed the war with great vigor as a member of the U.S. House of Representatives)—women were not the primary public spokespeople of these movements. Highly competent women did, however, play significant roles in the movements of the 1960s; they included Ella Baker, who still continues with her work for minority and feminist causes, and Faye Honey Knopp of the American Friends Service Committee, a founding member of NARMIC (National Action Research on the Military Industrial Complex). Knopp has more recently extended her energies to the prison reform movement.

In the 1960s and early 1970s radical political movements, women most frequently licked envelopes and washed dishes while the men planned strategy and gave speeches. A few black males found their way into the organizational structure of the antiwar movement, but for the most part blacks by the late 1960s were developing their own organizations, which they believed could most directly meet their needs.

Native Americans were seldom if ever incorporated into the decision-making structures of the 1960s political movements. But they began to seek a broader audience for their message based on respect for ancient sacred traditions and love of the earth.

Thomas Banyacya and other elders of the Hopi nation of the Southwest spoke eloquently of the Indian prophecies about the current need for humanity to purify itself. In Washington State, Sun Bear and Wabun started a new form of extended family, the Bear Tribe, in which those of all racial backgrounds are welcome. From the eastern tribes, Mad Bear Anderson and Medicine Story addressed the World Symposium on Humanity, held in Toronto in 1979.

Under the leadership of Cesar Chavez a heroic struggle has been waged to gain basic rights for millions of farmworkers. The campaigns of the United Farm Workers Union led to the California state legislature's 1975 guarantee of agricultural workers' rights to vote for a union of their choice for the first time in American history. Efforts to improve the generally poor living conditions for these (mainly Hispanic) workers continue.

Among the significant developments in the 1970s was the rapid expansion of the feminist movement. The quest for self-identity among women was explored and lucidly given voice by already established writers such as Adrienne Rich and Denise Levertov and by a goodly number of other talented and energetic novelists, poets, and artists.

One major focal point for many women in the 1970s was the struggle for ratification of the federal Equal Rights Amendment. Within a year after the ERA was passed by Congress in 1972, thirty states had ratified it. But a decade of hard work ended in frustration when time ran out for the required ratification by three-fourths of the state legislatures. Few issues have touched as deeply as the ERA, for it goes to the very core of how women and men view themselves and each other. Supporters of women's rights can justifiably point to the progress their movement made over the decade ending in 1982. They lost a battle, but the struggle goes on.

On the legal front feminists could point by 1982 to gains in federal equal-pay legislation, to laws requiring that public schools offer equal opportunities to both sexes, and to the fourteen states that added equal rights amendments to their constitutions. Political power is still badly skewed against them, but women have been entering politics at a greater rate than ever before, and their ranks in the state legislatures increased threefold from 1969 to 1982. Mobilized in such organizations as the National Organization for Women, women are becoming a considerable political force. New ground has been broken with the appointment of Sandra Day O'Connor to the Supreme Court, and the selection of Geraldine Ferraro as the Democratic vice-presidential candidate in 1984. Still, much remains to be done to secure justice for women, to gain equal employment opportunities and equal pay for equal work, and to rectify other more subtle forms of discrimination.

Women constitute the majority of those actively involved in the anti–nuclear weapons campaign and in human rights organizations such as Amnesty International. They also continue to perform much of the volunteer and social service work within their communities.

The feminist movement has helped many women gain a more positive sense of self-worth and has encouraged the development of mutual support networks. Attention has been focused on and organizations created to work against widespread sexual harassment and rape, and spouse and child abuse.

On the other hand, some of its strident language, especially in the earlier days of the women's liberation movement, played on the insecurities and fears of more conservative women, who later mobilized under Phyllis Schlafly to help defeat the ERA. Women who believe that being a good mother and homemaker is a vocation second in value to none felt undermined by their "liberated" sisters, who denigrated these traditional roles. Some of the extremism and posturing of the 1970s could be likened to a pendulum, which swings from side to side until it becomes centered. In the justifiable opposition to male chauvinism, it was inevitable that some of its female counterpart should emerge.

Women have had good reason to be angry, and an outpouring of pent-up feelings took place in the 1970s. Much of this energy is now directed to developing practicable means to combat sexism. The historic legacy of patriarchal dominance throughout almost all of the world is not easily rectified, but a start has been made, which will improve the quality of human relationships. Men, too, have been limited by sexist roles in the past and should welcome the freedom to develop fully the receptive, intuitive, and nurturing aspects of their nature.

To develop true equality and partnership between the sexes, the principle of inclusiveness needs to be enhanced. In her study *Androgyny,* June Singer speaks of the need to recognize and appreciate the universal human qualities within each gender of our species.[4] Women's liberation and its male counterpart each have significant contemporary roles to play, but out of this process perhaps a greater recognition of the need for *human* liberation and community will emerge.

Also characteristic of the reorientation in the 1970s was the desire to decentralize economic structures and make them more accessible. Elaborate organizational theories were avoided, and attention was focused on building at the grass-roots level. A large number of cooperatives sprang up across the country, especially consumer food co-ops. These new storefront co-ops are centers where people can get food at reasonable cost and come together socially. They also provide space for those who wish to learn more about natural foods, vegetarian options, and health care and often sponsor member-initiated classes or other activities.

In addition, the 1970s witnessed a resurgence of appreciation for products handcrafted with skill and care by people working in their homes or in small shops. HOME industries in Maine, mountain folk in Appalachia, and others banded together to market their goods so they could receive a fairer monetary return for them.

Some people during this period moved from urban to rural areas and farming. Others found jobs in rural or semirural areas and used their income to supplement large gardens and a few chickens, cows, or goats. Still others remained in their urban settings but began to reexamine their lives and relationships, and the use of their time, money, and energies.

The values indicated in the titles of E. F. Schumacher's books, *Small Is Beautiful: Economics As If People Mattered* and *Good Work,* challenge the stressful materialistic values of modern society. One important way to ease the strains of everyday life is to simplify. Through the ages certain people have chosen to live with a minimum of material possessions because such a life was consistent with their own sense of purpose, and because it set a positive example for others. The lives of Mother Teresa, Dorothy Day, and others whose work may not be as well known give a sense of the true meaning of selfless service.

It should be kept in mind that many of the 1970s "alternative life-styles" people have had economic and educational advantages that allow a considerable range of choice. Opting for a life of voluntary simplicity is of course far different from choosing grinding poverty.

An increasing number of people are becoming aware, however, of the implications arising from the fact that we Americans consume an estimated one-third of the world's goods and services. Surveys conducted by Gallup, Harris, Daniel Yankelovich, and others point to millions of Americans who in the 1970s began to move away from the old models of success, measured in terms of status and material acquisition and consumption.[5] Learning to cut back on the nonessentials will ease the current imbalance between the haves and have-nots while helping to bring a conscientious quality into daily living situations.

Support has grown for ecologically based movements, which strive to preserve the natural environment. This concern is expressed in the generalized opposition to nuclear power and in the advocacy of renewable, nonpolluting energy sources drawn from the sun, the wind, the waves, and the earth itself. Environmental groups such as Greenpeace and Friends of the Earth have focused on preserving all living creatures on this planet, and the Paul Winter Consort has celebrated these endangered species in its music.

In the words of a Joni Mitchell song, "they've paved Paradise and put up a parking lot." Even in the world of concrete though, Pete Seeger's perennial optimism called our attention to the "grass which grows up between the cracks in the pavement." For decades he has given benefit concerts on behalf of the poor and the exploited, and for peace. In the 1970s Seeger and friends sailed up and down the polluted Hudson River in the *Clearwater*, an old sloop they had restored. At concerts and get-togethers along the riverbanks they mobilized local residents to help clean up the once beautiful waterway and return it to a healthy condition.

Other musicians including Harry Chapin, Phil Ochs, John Lennon, Malvina Reynolds, Joan Baez, Dizzy Gillespie, and Arlo Guthrie gave freely of their time and energy to support a variety of social and environmental causes.

Self-Exploration and Spirituality

In the 1970s there developed an increased interest in exploring ways to realize human potential and find out more about "what makes the inner self tick." The panaceas put forth to meet this new market were often superficial or played on people's insecurities. It soon occurs to the serious student that "life made easy" books offer limited returns at best, and that one's benefits from any endeavor are proportionate to the sincere effort one puts into it. The search for self-knowledge and purpose in life is long, and there are few easy answers.

Taking an active role in the maintenance of one's health, utilizing preventative medicine, and becoming better informed about basic nutrition are part of this trend. The approaches of chiropractic, naturopathy, homeopathy, nutritional therapy, applied kinesiology, and the Oriental-based healing arts of acupressure and shiatsu are being further explored to balance out the overdominant allopathic medical system, with its excessive reliance on treatment through synthetic drugs and surgery. The use of natural herbs, relaxation techniques, and meditation to develop and maintain good health is becoming more widespread. Much-needed attention is being given to learning what good health really is about, and to finding a harmonious balance of body, mind, and spirit. A "total person concept" of health involves understanding the connection between a person's mental, biochemical, and structural conditions. All these approaches share the premise that each person should take more responsibility for his or her own health and education.

Books such as *Our Bodies, Ourselves* indicate the strides women have taken to gain more control over their physical well-being.

The widespread natural childbirth movement and home birth with the assistance of trained midwives give expectant mothers additional alternatives. Prodded by these developments, some hospitals have opened improved "birthing centers," and more obstetricians are using the Leboyer method of delivery.

Crafts and music provide other useful and enjoyable modes of getting in touch with oneself. Yoga, tai chi, and jogging became popular in the 1970s, and "zen and the art of . . ." books appeared on everything from archery and tennis to motorcycle maintenance.

A plethora of approaches to self-awareness came to the fore. They involve both highly structured systems and simple methods to help practitioners better understand their own minds and bodies. These include biofeedback, psychosynthesis, various forms of meditation, and dream therapy. People often work together in mutual self-help, encounter, and study groups. Simultaneous with the emphasis on doing things naturally is a decrease of interest in artificially induced "highs"—the centering and self-development approaches of the 1970s offered more controlled, sustainable, and less potentially dangerous means to consciousness raising than the "mind-expanding" drugs of the 1960s.

In the 1960s and 1970s serious questioning took place in many American churches and synagogues. Attendance sometimes declined in the process, but those who remained were often strengthened in their convictions. Small groups, generally of people in their twenties and thirties, broke away from larger, established congregations and formed their own fellowships. In Judaism, for example, the Havurot movement, which began in several northeastern cities, sought to deepen personal religious understanding and cultural bonds within the framework of close-knit community.

The Negro freedom struggle in the 1950s had its roots in southern black churches. Significant support for the civil rights movement subsequently developed among Jewish and Christian liberals, primarily in the North. International developments reflected similar trends. In Latin America the concept of liberation theology gained support in lower echelons of the Church as a Christian response to the crying need of the poor for social justice. Meanwhile, in Europe formal dialogue was initiated between Christians and Marxists.

Another significant development in the 1970s was the rapid growth of the "born-again" movement in Christianity, especially among fundamentalists and charismatics. By the close of the decade, an estimated 35 million Americans referred to themselves as born again, including all three major presidential candidates in the 1980 elections—Ronald Reagan, Jimmy Carter, and John Anderson. To be "reborn" has different levels of meaning to various people, but a direct and personal experience is common. Many have testified to the beneficial effects of "accepting Jesus as their personal savior."

Fundamentalists have taken advantage of television and radio to spread their message. On Sunday mornings and increasingly throughout the week a plethora of preachers—usually white, southern, male, and politically conservative—put forth their interpretations of the gospel to millions of viewers and listeners. Through the rubric of the Moral Majority a substantial number of fundamentalist clergy have become increasingly involved in the support of right-wing political causes.

For some fundamentalists, the influx of non-Western influences represents the "devious handiwork of the Antichrist." This belief is fueled by the notoriety generated by the activities of a few sects, most notably the Reverend Sun Myung Moon's Unification Church, which, ironically purports to be Christian.

Along with the rapidly expanding post–World War II commercial contact between Asia and the United States came yoga; the Oriental martial and healing arts; meditative techniques; Eastern music; the *I Ching;* the book of Tao; and various forms of Hindu, Buddhist, Sikh, Sufi, Islamic, and other religious and philosophical practices. This cultural influx first arrived on the West Coast, most notably in California, and its influence spread to the East Coast and then to parts of the Midwest. In the 1960s writers such as D. T. Suzuki and Alan Watts interpreted and helped to popularize traditional Oriental practices which in the past had been available to relatively few people. By the 1970s these Eastern influences had gained a considerable impact on those seeking to grow in self-understanding and to "expand their consciousness." Scholars such as Jacob Needleman and Harvey Cox have written perceptively of the forms that various Asian traditions have taken in America, and of the attraction of these religions to their adherents.[6] Cox reminds his readers of both "the promise and the peril of the New Orientalism." It is interesting that in a literal sense the word *reorientation* suggests a return to the Orient. A number of those who went through a period of reflection, asking basic questions about the meaning and direction of their lives, turned to the East in their quest for understanding. This was not just a historic coincidence, for Asia, ranging geographically from Jerusalem to Japan, is the cradle of many of the world's major religious and spiritual traditions. The "new seekers" wanted to become more centered or whole—thus the popularization of the term *holistic,* which stems from the same root as the word *holy.*

In circumnavigating the planet, one ultimately reaches the West by sailing east. Similarly, by learning something of the roots of non-Western traditions, it becomes easier to get one's bearings and develop a new perspective on our Western heritage. Likewise, some in contemporary Asia draw inspiration from sociopolitical ideas (those of Locke, Jefferson, Marx, and others) and from the scientific revolution that originated in the West.

The shrinkage of the globe through science and technology necessitates a greater awareness of human interdependence. And this interdependence in the outer world corresponds to each person's inner world. The East can be seen in the Jungian sense as a metaphor for the intuitive, reflective, receptive, nurturing part of the human psyche. The West can symbolize the active, assertive, rational components. The political goal of reconciliation among the world's people is linked with the psychological need to achieve a greater integration within the individual.

The more significant aspects of a personal spiritual quest are generally removed from public view. Serious students may seek insight in the teachings and lives of twentieth-century Eastern sages such as Sri Aurobindo, Sant Kirpal Singh, Hazrat Inayat Khan, Paramhansa Yogananda, and Shaunryu Suzuki, as well as the historic traditions. In addition, many have read the writings of fellow Westerners who have turned eastward for inspiration; they include Alice Bailey, Roshi Kennett, and Ram Dass (Richard Alpert). Still others study with Americans trained in the Eastern sacred traditions such as Sensei Bernie Glassman, a former mathematician who now heads the New York Zendo. There are, in addition, followers of Western distillations of ancient teachings that form the basis of such practices as psychosynthesis and actualism.

Less-known traditions of the East, such as Sufism and Sant Mat (The Path of the Saints), are now coming to the attention of more sincere seekers. Interest has also grown in the deeper meaning of the mystic Christian traditions and in the Christian writings that span the centuries from Meister Eckhart and St. Teresa to Pierre Teilhard de Chardin and Thomas Merton. From the Jewish heritage come the insights of the Torah, Kabbalah, and the great Hasidic rabbis. And the profound respect for the "Great Spirit" and the forces of nature in the traditions of native peoples of Africa and America has been another source of inspiration and learning.

Despite their outer differences, seekers exploring these traditions have in common a quest for self-understanding and what has been described in terms such as *enlightenment* or *God-realization*. Such an endeavor has, of course, long been a part of the Western experience, as evidenced by the writings of Blake, Emerson, the transcendentalists, and Whitman, among others.

The esoteric teachings touch people's lives and bring them together in the recognition that beneath all surface differences and doctrinal forms exists a fundamental unity of humankind. There is a sense of being together on a spiritual path, a "path with heart." While pursuing one's own way, one gains an increasing awareness of the validity of others' experiences, including those of professed agnostics and atheists. Some who have been influenced by non-Western teachings have rediscovered or deepened their own roots in Christianity or Judaism. They have found renewed meaning in coming back to the West after first turning East.

Critics of the "Me" generation have rightfully called attention to the superficial aspects of "turning inward," and to the self-centeredness of some who have joined the less creditable human potential or religious groups. The emphasis on putting oneself first frequently leads to lack of concern for others. And the religious quest itself can subtly degenerate into spiritual materialism. The goal of all these teachings, however, is identifying with other human beings and being of service to society. Anyone who studies their basic intent eventually learns that there is no place for self-obsession or selfishness.

One problem with "turning eastward" stems from the fact that many of the traditional spiritual paths arose historically in settings substantially different from the West. Transplanting and adapting these traditions sometimes leads to misunderstandings. And within religious as well as political movements the danger has always existed that charismatic leaders can combine authoritarian religion and politics in distorted movements that attract mindless followers.

Excesses in large organizations purporting to provide enlightenment techniques (for a "modest price") also exist in our consumer-oriented society. Such groups most often become the focus of public attention, while the quieter, less flamboyant ones remain generally unknown.

Reintegrating Knowledge and Life

An increasing number of people are coming to the understanding that science, religion, philosophy, and art are all branches of a common tree. An integrative and unifying body of knowledge based on this recognition is being developed, which can serve as an antidote to the sense of compartmentalization and separation that is often fostered in the educational systems of an overspecialized society. In metaphysics, for example, the notion of an integrated "world philosophy" is being developed. Based originally on the work of Swiss philosopher Jean Gebser, this approach draws on the historic and contemporary thought and wisdom of all the world's cultures, not only those of the Western philosophic traditions.

In the 1970s the links between science and spirituality were elucidated in the work of physicists including Austrian-born Fritjof Capra of the University of California (Berkeley) and David Bohm of Great Britain. In his widely read *The Tao of Physics,* Capra explores the parallels between modern physics and Eastern mysticism. He concludes that "science does not need mysticism and mysticism does not need science; but humanity needs both. Mystical experience is necessary to understand the deepest nature of things and science is essential for human life." Demonstrating this contention, he points to and graphically illustrates the marked similarity between the movement of subatomic particles and the traditional "dances of life" depicted in various art forms.[7]

David Bohm has developed holographic models to help visualize the notion of an "implicate order," which links and enfolds all of "Reality." He submits that ultimately each person is connected to the totality of the life-force in the universe.[8]

The 1970s also saw significant breakthroughs in the exploration of extraterrestial space. In 1969 Americans set foot on the moon, and in later years space vehicles probed the planets from Venus to Saturn, sending back remarkably beautiful and revealing photographs. Many of the astronauts have been deeply moved by their experiences, and several have had significant life changes thereafter. Edgar Mitchell, for example, founded the Noetics Institute for the study of science and human consciousness.

It has finally dawned on some Hollywood scriptwriters and producers that "outer-space creatures" need not be portrayed as menacing. For the first time the public has been treated to films like *Close Encounters of the Third Kind* and *E.T.* to help balance out other fear-inducing movies.

Dealing with the relationship between life and death has generally been a taboo in American society. The work of Drs. Elisabeth Kübler-Ross and Mwalimu Imaru and their associates is especially valuable and leads to a clearer understanding of the often debilitating phenomenon of grief.[9] Studies by Dr. Philip Moody, *Life after Life,* and Dr. Kenneth Ring, *Life at Death,* provide accounts of illuminating visions by hundreds of people from many backgrounds who have undergone near-death experiences. These investigations help generate increased understanding of the links between the oft-polarized fields of science and religion.[10]

The 1970s were thus a time for substantial growth in various areas of human understanding. Although there were considerable excesses in what sociologist Theodore Roszak has called the "consciousness carnival," a new era of serious exploration into the far reaches of inner space had begun.

Notes

1. This time of reassessment is discussed in considerable detail by Patricia Hunt-Perry and Arthur Stein in "Seeds of Change, A Time of Reorientation," *Phoenix: Journal of Transpersonal Anthropology,* vol. 5, no. 1 (1981): 67–78.

2. *A Guide to Cooperative Alternatives* (New Haven, Conn., and Louisa, Va.: Community Publications Cooperative, 1969). First conceived by Paul Freundlich, the guide sought to pull together information on "all the separate strands which make up the rich texture of the cooperative fabric."

3. See Peter Clecak, *America's Quest for the Ideal Self: Dissent and Fulfillment in the 6os and 7os* (New York: Oxford University Press, 1983).

4. June Singer, *Androgyny: Towards a New Theory of Sexuality* (New York: Doubleday, Anchor, 1976).

5. See, for example, Daniel Yankelovich, *New Rules* (New York: Random House, 1981).

6. Harvey Cox, *Turning East: The Promise and Peril of the New Orientalism* (New York: Simon and Schuster, 1977); and Jacob Needleman, *The New Religions* (New York: Doubleday, 1970).

7. Fritjof Capra, *The Tao of Physics* (New York: Bantam, 1977).

8. David Bohm, *Wholeness and the Implicate Order* (Boston: Routledge and Kegan Paul, 1980).

9. Elisabeth Kübler-Ross's best-known book is *On Death and Dying* (New York: Macmillan, 1969).

10. Philip Moody, *Life after Life* (Tallahassee: Mockingbird Press, 1975); and Kenneth Ring, *Life at Death: A Scientific Investigation of the Near-Death Experience* (New York: Coward, McCann and Geoghegan, 1980).

Chapter 2

Seeking Renewal in Rural America

In the 1970s several hundred thousand people, primarily in their twenties and thirties, were attracted by the idea of going "back to the land." Most were from white, middle-class family backgrounds, and many were college educated. This chapter begins with a discussion of the lives and philosophy of Scott and Helen Nearing, who served as role models for a number of the new homesteaders, and then looks at the experiences of Wendell Berry and of a couple who have successfully homesteaded in Maine. The later sections of the chapter will focus on the much larger number of rural Americans who lack educational opportunities and mobility and sometimes do not own the land on which they work. I will describe several ongoing projects, which, though diverse, concur that the poor are best served by being helped to achieve economic self-sufficiency. These experiments in cooperation offer positive alternatives for earning a sustainable income, promoting human dignity, and developing a purposeful community life.

The Nearings—Modern American Pioneers

Self-reliance has been linked with democracy in the American mind since Thomas Jefferson extolled the small farmer as the cornerstone of a free society.[1] Henry David Thoreau spoke of similar values. In our day, Scott and Helen Nearing have epitomized the best of that tradition.

Born in 1883 into a prosperous, politically conservative Pennsylvania family, Scott Nearing studied and taught economics until his increasingly radical views and his outspokenness about child labor got him fired from the University of Pennsylvania's Wharton School of Business.

As a leading spokesman for the Socialist Party, Nearing opposed America's entrance into World War I. By 1920 his political views had cost him another professorship, and he had been prosecuted (unsuccessfully) under the Espionage Act for giving encouragement to draft resisters. For a short time in the late 1920s he was a member of the American Communist Party, but he was soon expelled from it too for being too outspoken and not submitting to party discipline. Thus, by 1930, his free thinking had made Nearing unacceptable to orthodox capitalists and Communists alike.

Around that time he met Helen Knothe, daughter of a prominent New Jersey manufacturer, and soon they were married. Twenty years younger than Scott, Helen was a gifted student of the violin, had traveled widely in Europe and Asia, and as an active member of the Theosophical Society was an occasional companion of J. Krishnamurti and Annie Besant. When Scott found himself unable to get his writings published and often refused permission to speak at public forums, the Nearings decided that "we would rather be poor in the country than poor in the city." They left their cold-water flat in New York City to begin a new way of life.

In the Depression economy of the mid-1930s, the Nearings found a rundown, seventy-three-acre farm in rural Vermont, which they purchased for $300 down and an $800 mortgage. They drew up a plan described in *Living the Good Life: How to Live Sanely and Safely in a Troubled World:* "to set up a semi-self-contained household unit, based largely on a use economy, and as far as possible, independent of the price-profit economy which surrounds us."[2]

The Nearings sought out literature, some dating back several hundred years, on land care and on nearly forgotten skills such as building stone walls. They used only organic materials for fertilizer and developed simple but effective composting techniques. Soon they had a thriving garden, which provided them with an assortment of fresh vegetables, including greens they learned to grow through much of the harsh New England winter. They brought the tired old farm to life, developed maple syruping as a cash crop, and over the years constructed a number of impressive buildings, primarily from the native stone on the land.

The Nearings organized their daily lives so they had time not only for "bread labor" but also to pursue their intellectual, artistic, and recreational interests. They viewed their physical work not as toil but rather as a pleasurable and creative means to earn an honest livelihood. They preferred whenever possible to use hand tools, which they felt were an extension of themselves. Well before the energy crisis, they confined their use of nonrenewable fossil fuels to an occasional use of an old truck.

Their keys to good health were basic and straightforward: eating a simple vegetarian diet, getting plenty of fresh air, doing lots of productive labor for exercise, going to sleep by 9:00 P.M. and awakening before sunrise, and maintaining a positive mental attitude. Their overall health improved considerably as they adapted to the rigors of homesteading. Over a half-century they rarely needed to call on a doctor. Once, when asked if he had life insurance, Scott Nearing replied with a chuckle, "No, I practice it." Only when his body literally wore down from old age and he was confined to a wheelchair at the age of ninety-eight did he reluctantly give up his yearly chore of cutting six cords of firewood.

While living in Vermont and later in Maine, Scott continued to do research and to write, and over the years he and Helen published about fifty books and pamphlets themselves, because no academic or commercial press would accept his writings. He was also a regular contributor for several decades to the *Monthly Review,* an independent socialist journal based in New York City. During the winters the Nearings often traveled and lectured in the United States and abroad. Over the years they visited all fifty states. Scott continued to see himself as a teacher. While denied a formal classroom, he was not constricted, for he defined a teacher as "one who seeks the truth, spreads the truth, and tries to incorporate the truth into the life of the human community." In addition to his political and economic treatises, Scott collaborated with Helen on a series of accounts about their homesteading experiences, beginning with the *Maple Syrup Book* (1951).

The Nearings learned some basic skills from their neighbors in the early years and made barter arrangements for work and produce. Attempts at other forms of cooperative endeavor did not work out. Scott eventually came to realize that most old-time Vermonters were not receptive, to put it mildly, to his leftist political thinking. The Sunday afternoon musical sessions at their home, which Helen initiated, were more successful.

In 1951, when nearby Stratton Mountain was turned into a ski resort, the Nearings moved from Vermont to Maine. They paid $7,500 for 140 acres of an overgrown farm on the central Maine coast at Harborside, overlooking Penobscot Bay. With the help of friends and neighbors, they eventually built a handsome stone house (on which Helen did all the masonry). Their home is simply furnished and has such innovative features as a clivus multrum, a composting toilet to recycle both human and kitchen organic waste material. The old house on the property was turned into a center for the Small Farms Research Organization, which offers short courses on organic gardening.

In Maine the Nearings concentrated on learning about soils and plant life, and finding ways for people to live more harmoniously in their natural surroundings. They also continued to share their practical experiences. Scott, for example, wrote a book about greenhouse farming in the winter without the use of artificial heating. Helen compiled a cookbook that draws on the couple's practice of eating food that is "as unprocessed as possible, as fresh from the garden as possible, as little cooked as

possible, and non-flesh." The couple took on various speaking
engagements and attended conferences sponsored by groups such
as the Maine Organic Farmers.

At a time in their lives when most Americans are well past
retirement, the Nearings continued to be actively engaged in
productive work. For more than twenty-five years they labored
to convert a swampy acre on their land into a pond. They carted
away more than 16,000 wheelbarrow loads of silt from the area,
which they used for mulching fruit trees, for composting, and
in the greenhouse. For the Nearings, the "tiny postage-stamp
pond is a miniature reclamation project which offers us exercise
in its construction, irrigation, sods, topsoil, ice to skate on in
Winter and a major asset in case of fire. We began our work
on the pond in 1953. Twenty-five years later we are still excavat-
ing, deepening, enlarging."

In the 1960s and 1970s, Forest Farm, as their Maine home is
called, was visited by thousands who had read the Nearings'
books. It wasn't always easy for the couple to accommodate visitors and still maintain their daily activities, so their visitors were
soon put to work. At mealtimes or around the fireplace in the
evening there was time for response to questions and sometimes
a good-natured exchange of anecdotes and stories. The Nearings
sold some of their land at a minimal price to several young
families who had come to live and work with them.

Living the Good Life, which the Nearings first published and
distributed in 1954 through their Social Science Institute Press,
sold at best a few thousand copies a year. The fact that it became
a best-seller when republished by Shocken Books in 1970 was an
encouraging sign of the new interest in alternative ways of life.
Scott's political autobiography, *The Making of a Radical,* also
sold well after being reissued by Harper and Row in 1972.

In 1973 Scott's alma mater, the University of Pennsylvania,
which had ousted him from its faculty fifty-eight years earlier,
named him honorary professor of economics. The citation
praised him "for adhering to a belief that to seek out and to
teach the truth is life's highest aim." He was also sought out for
television and magazine interviews; he joked that perhaps all
the attention indicated he was getting too soft in his social criti-

cism. In any event, he claimed that some nationally prominent newspapers still refused to carry ads for his self-published *Civilization and Beyond* (1975).

Among those most critical of the Nearings are some political activists who say that those committed to radical change should not have removed themselves to a pastoral, rural area. Then there are life-style purists who say the Nearings were not completely self-sufficient; they bought some items in the store and even had an electric freezer in the cellar of their Maine home. It is also accurately pointed out that the Nearings could not have had so much personal freedom and time to travel if they had had children or raised animals.

But although the Nearings sought to be as self-sufficient as possible, they did not make self-sufficiency a fetish. They recognized that people are interdependent and that it is appropriate to exchange some goods and services. They also acknowledged that their life-style is obviously not for everyone, and that reasonably priced land is not nearly as available as it once was. But the principles to which they adhered—using time resourcefully, earning an honest livelihood, working cooperatively, living simply—can be applied by people anywhere.

The Nearings were perfectionists who over time learned to accept their limitations. Essentially serious minded, they developed a sense of humor and playfulness with each other that served them well in their later years. In the summer of 1983, at the age of one hundred, Scott Nearing died peacefully at home.

Living a Good Life, Country-style

Like the Nearings, the poet-scholar-farmer Wendell Berry speaks eloquently of the intrinsic value of combining intellectual and manual work. Berry teaches English at the University of Kentucky, and he and his wife and children also maintain the farm where four generations of his family have lived. In his twenty-five books of fiction, essays, and poetry runs the theme that we need to make the connections between life and love and food and work.

Recently a U.S. government official marveled that 95 percent of all Americans are "freed from the drudgery of providing their own food." Behind this statement lies a belief, shared by many, that physical work is distasteful and undesirable. Berry believes that this widespread attitude has led to the abuse of land itself—farmers are seen as miners of the topsoil rather than nurturers of the land. The resultant soil crisis is threatening the very life and productivity of America's finest farmland. In *The Unsettling of America* Berry writes: "The fields lose their humus and porosity (through erosion), become less retentive of water, depend more on pesticides, herbicides, chemical fertilizers. Bigger tractors become necessary because the compacted soils are harder to work—and their greater weight further compacts the soil." He cites estimates that "it now costs (by erosion) two bushels of Iowa topsoil to grow one bushel of corn."[3]

As his family's farm experiences unavoidable erosion caused by periodic flooding of the nearby Kentucky River, Berry views his stewardship of the land partly as a reclamation project. He and his wife also share the belief that no vocation is more important than being fully attentive to the responsibilities of parenthood. He draws together the links between nurturing the land and nurturing children in one of his recent essays, "Family Work," in *The Gift of Good Land:*

> For those of us who have wished to raise our food and our children at home, it is easy enough to state the idea. Growing our own food, unlike buying it, is a complexity, and it affects deeply the shape and value of our lives. We like the thought that the outdoor work that improves our health should produce food of excellent quality that, in turn, also improves and safeguards our health. We like no less the thought that the home production of food can improve the quality of family life. Not only do we intend to give our children better food than we can buy for them at the store, or than they will buy for themselves from vending machines or burger joints; we also know that growing and preparing food at home can provide family work—work for everybody. And by thus elaborating household chores and obligations, we hope to strengthen the bonds of interest, loyalty, affection and cooperation that keep families together.[4]

Part of the motivation for the back-to-the-land movement of the 1970s was the promise of clean air and honest work, of rediscovering personal roots, and of developing self-reliance. Part also had to do with getting away from the problems of urban

America and creating a less materialistic life-style. Many of the new homesteaders went to such rural areas as northern New England, the Ozarks, and the Pacific Northwest, where land was still relatively inexpensive and accessible. Some found it difficult to obtain the kind of land they wanted—there is less arable land available today and it costs considerably more than when the Nearings first went to Vermont. Others found that their romantic notions about living in the country or the mountains were soon tempered by the hard work and day-to-day realities. Nor was rural or small town life a panacea for all personal problems. Some left the land after a year or two, chastened but perhaps wiser.

But many of those who moved to rural America in the 1970s stayed and built a new life for themselves. It takes planning, the capacity to adjust, persistence, resourcefulness, and a sense of humor to succeed. But where there is a will, there is a way.

One young couple, Harvey Lorber and Gloria Banasch, left Rhode Island to live on an undeveloped piece of land they had purchased twenty miles from Bangor, Maine. Living in the back of their Volkswagen van during the first winter, they planted a garden when springtime came and cleared away enough trees for a homesite and workshop area. Over ten years they expanded their original self-built, one-room dwelling with loft into a large, solar-heated home complete with a sunken greenhouse in the living room and a clivus maximus in the basement, which recycles all organic waste materials from the bathroom and kitchen. In the "front yard" they converted a swampy area into a swimable fish pond complete with a little waterfall.

Their first years in Maine were spent partly in developing basic skills and earning a subsistence living. When old friends asked them what they were doing, they replied, "Just living in Maine," implying that simply sustaining a new life there was a full-time occupation. With the skills developed in building his own home, Lorber now helps others, including old-time Maine residents, build their own inexpensive, functional, and aesthetically pleasing homes. He has offered a course on the subject at the Extension Division of the University of Maine and also facilitates the building of solar greenhouses that can be constructed over a weekend by small groups of people in the old "barn-raising tradition. In addition to her construction, homemaking, gardening, and caring for the animals, Banasch has worked in several outside teaching positions with the mentally or emotionally handicapped.

Lorber and Banasch share most aspects of their life, and like many other newcomers to homesteading life, they had to prove to themselves that they "could do it on their own" and meet the many challenges that a rural life-style presented. But after five or six years, when they had secured their basic needs, they began to look for something more than subsistence. Others who had come to Maine in the late 1960s and early 1970s also felt the necessity to broaden the scope of their lives. Starting with discussion groups and a cooperative garden, they and their friends in the region began to attempt to do more in common. Disillusioned by Vietnam and Watergate, they had eschewed politics, but by the late 1970s a number of the newer Maine settlers had gotten involved in local political and social issues and helped elect a progressive, conservation-minded Congressman.

Self-Help Projects for the Rural Poor

Those described thus far in this chapter have much to teach about self-reliance. They are well-educated individuals who have voluntarily chosen their life-style. But what about the poor, those with little educational opportunity and mobility, who are often trapped in their poverty?

In the 1970s an encouraging trend developed from Maine through Appalachia to Georgia—people coming together to market their home-crafted products collectively, obtain land, exchange goods and services, and disseminate training and information. These groups include HOME in Maine, Koinonia in Georgia, the Rural Advancement Fund, the National Sharecroppers Fund, New Communities Incorporated, and the Institute for International Economics.

Home Workers Organized for More Employment (HOME) was started by local people in Orland, along the coast of Maine, in 1970 to improve their living conditions. More specifically, HOME began when Sister Lucy Poulin responded to a destitute woman's request to help her sell her crafts.

In one of the poorest regions of the country, where more than one of four people are dependent on welfare, HOME has enabled its members to achieve more economic self-sufficiency. Local women had previously sold most of their fine home-crafted goods to outside purchasers who, in turn, retailed them at large markups in the Boston and New York areas. However, the development through HOME of self-run, community-based marketing outlets led to a revival of cottage industries as a viable source of income.

The money received from their crafts cooperatives has made the difference between basic survival and some measure of comfort and dignity for hundreds of families. Cooperative outlet shops for craft and farm products opened in a number of towns through the region. In Orland itself a cluster of community workshops has been built for leather working, weaving, ceramics, woodworking, and other crafts. Pooling their resources has enabled the members to acquire good-quality tools and other needed equipment. Instead of working in isolation in their homes, women can come together in a pleasant environment. Young children attend the day-care center and little school in the compound, and their mothers can spend time with them during the day. The boys and girls see their parents at work and gain firsthand knowledge about their skilled techniques. Some men have joined the craft cooperatives as well.

The organization and good spirit of the HOME center in Orland are impressive. A large gift shop displays and sells the products made by HOME workers, and exhibitions and demonstrations are held on everything from churning butter to spinning cloth. Visitors can also gain an appreciation of the skills involved by watching craftspeople at work in their shops.

Continuing education classes are held at some of the centers. In the Bangor area at one point in the late 1970s, about 400 people ranging in age from sixteen to sixty-five were attending classes on a variety of subjects. Among these, eighty who had never completed school were working to get their high-school diplomas. Sometimes three generations of the same family took part in the tutoring and high-school equivalency education.

HOME also has developed programs to help people obtain land, build houses, grow food, and raise livestock in a region where construction costs and land prices would otherwise be prohibitively high. George McRobie, who visited HOME in 1978 at the beginning of a cross-country exploration of alternative technologies, described the HOME land trust, Self-Help Family Farms, in his excellent book *Small Is Possible:*

By leasing land from the trust, a poor family can get a farm on the understanding that they will contribute their labor to the building of other people's homes. In this way energy-efficient houses have been built costing $10,000 or less. Low monthly payments cover mortgage, taxes, insurance, and land rents. The trust is now exploring the possibilities of community investment: thus, say, $100,000 donated to H.O.M.E. could be repaid in ten years by small farmers who could be settled with the aid of this money and grow timber as a cash crop for purposes of repayment.[5]

Through the St. Francis Community, HOME also has helped elderly and destitute families to obtain wood fuel in the cold winters. Volunteer labor has been provided to build homes for the neediest families. Some of those who work at HOME live together in the St. Francis Community—they also practice a craft, grow their own food, and cut wood in the forest for fuel and lumber.

An article in *Peacework* reported that in 1981 HOME set up a five-year plan to build thirty-two more family farms for some of the most vulnerable families in the St. Francis Community area. Also planned are a sawmill and shingle mill to process wood used in the houses, another craft store, and a cheese processing plant to create work for the unemployed. By providing an outlet for marginal farms, the cheese plant will also help revive the local farm economy.[6]

Similarly the biracial Koinonia community in rural Georgia is self-sustaining. Koinonia is a nondenominational Christian community in which whites and blacks have lived and worked together harmoniously for forty years in the racially troubled Deep South.[7] Its main source of income is homegrown pecans and products like pecan pies, which are sold in several parts of the country by supportive groups. For example, the Arlington Street Church in Boston, long known for promoting peace and racial equality, provides an outlet for Koinonia products and handicrafts made by the rural poor of Appalachia.

The Rural Advancement Fund (RAF) has helped small farmers in the South in their ongoing struggles to stay on the land in the face of expanding agribusiness and the rapid decline of the nation's small-farm sector. By developing improved agricultural practices, small farmers can better withstand the host of economic problems with which they are confronted. One innovative RAF program is a paraprofessional school at the Frank Porter Graham Center in North Carolina. In cooperation with VISTA's ACTION Program, RAF is training small farmers from the Carolinas to be farm improvement workers and community organizers. Selected for their potential leadership qualities, these trainees gain technical, agricultural, and community development skills. After five months of intensive study, they return home and share their newly acquired knowledge with farming neighbors and nearby communities. Their work will help establish a network of farmers through a wide range of rural communities.[8]

Participants in the program are men and women of varying ages, including whites, blacks, and Native Americans. Some are relative newcomers to farming; others have a lifetime of farming experience behind them. The first "graduating class" of seventeen small farmers recruited from eight counties in North and South Carolina completed their training in 1980. They are now assisting neighbors with their gardens. Many are working with local farmers to increase productivity while cutting back on costly chemicals. Others are helping organize farmers' markets and small-scale cooperatives. Some are teaching reading and conducting classes in skills to earn extra income. Using their own farms as demonstrations, these women and men will share their knowledge of passive solar greenhouses, organically grown vegetables, herb gardening, and recycled livestock housing. Their work will bring people together and create a better life for themselves and their neighbors and communities.

An important RAF effort in 1980 was combating adult illiteracy. It may sound improbable in a country that has prided itself on its educational achievements, but an estimated 20 million adult Americans are functionally illiterate (unable to read at a fifth-grade level). Illiteracy fosters unemployment and is deeply frustrating to those who cannot read. It results in less income and, thereby, a lower tax base for the community as a whole.

The greatest concentration of illiteracy is in the rural South. In Anson County, North Carolina, where the Frank Graham Center is located, 58 percent of the adult population was identified in 1970 as functionally illiterate. An adult program was begun focusing on techniques for teaching others to read. A number of those trained by the RAF-VISTA program are now setting up literacy programs in their communities.

In addition to being given reading lessons, nonreaders are helped to overcome their feelings of alienation and to become more actively involved in their communities. One of the most successful approaches is the "Each One Teach One" method, which promotes learning on a one-to-one basis.

Other VISTA trainees are addressing the immediate problems resulting from the worsening economic situation and the cutback of federal aid by the Reagan administration. Food pantries, used clothing centers, and crisis funds have been set up. Through farmers' markets these programs are also benefiting urban consumers, who are getting better-quality food at more reasonable prices.

According to the annual report by Kathryn Waller, the energetic executive director of RAF, projects in 1981 included women's workshops designed to teach self-reliance through developing economic viability and basic survival skills. "Each workshop concentrated on different topics such as new skills for generating extra income; small-scale, energy-saving solar additions to house and farm; growing and preserving food; and organic gardening. All the workshops combined 'hands-on' training with a sharing of ideas and experiences."[9]

Numerous requests were received to conduct similar workshops outside the region. Appalachian women in Tennessee and Kentucky were reached through Mountain Women's Exchange. Through the National Association of Farmworker Organizations, a workshop was provided for migrant farm workers in New Jersey. And, with the cooperation of the Southern Mutual Self-Help Association, several weeks were spent with sugarcane workers in the bayou country of Louisiana, focusing on energy-saving solar technology and efficient food production and preservation techniques.

In 1981 the RAF also gave attention to substandard housing—which is a grim reality for many rural poor in the South. One effort involved refurbishing sharecropper houses. As a demonstration project, an old house was "recycled" into a viable option for efficient, low-cost rural housing. The National Sharecroppers Fund (NSF) was first organized to support the struggles of the Southern Tenant Farmers Union, a biracial group of tenant farmers and sharecroppers founded in Arkansas in 1934. Since then it has helped tenant farmers upgrade their often deplorable economic conditions and acquire land for themselves and their families.

The NSF is also committed on both the national and international levels to permitting the free flow of botanical genetic information.[10] In the United States many independent seed companies have been bought out by large corporations. For example, Burpee Seeds is now owned by International Telephone and Telegraph. These corporations, in attempting to maximize their profits, have been promoting congressional legislation that would allow patents on seeds. This practice has already led to the extinction of a large number of traditional varieties of seeds. It also presents a dangerous trend toward future genetic conformity in plants.

In October 1981 the NSF hosted a unique conference that offered practical training in seed conservation. It brought together individuals and organizations who had made valuable contributions to national seed conservation—a "seed-savers network" that will continue to play an active role in educational and political campaigns for genetic conservation.

At the United Nations Food and Agricultural Organization
(FAO) Conference held in Rome in November 1981, the NSF
lobbied successfully for a resolution providing for the establish-
ment of an international seed bank which would guarantee access
to germ plasm material [seeds] for all nations, without regard to
politics. Such international cooperation is essential. The resolution is designed to protect the world's genetic resources and make
this common heritage of humankind available to plant breeders
and researchers of all countries. Before the FAO conference, the
NSR's Gary Fowler spoke and led workshops at meetings of
citizens representing farm, environmental, church, and public
interest groups from North and South America, Europe, Africa,
and Asia.

In the United States the NSF stood alone when it initiated its
campaign to block bills permitting an expansion of seed patent-
ing. But many environmental, agricultural, and other organizations have since joined in this cause, and support has also come
from increasing numbers of leading academics and researchers.
The problem is an ongoing one and far from resolved, however.
At stake is the protection of genetic resources that are essential
to life at all levels.

Rural poverty is a continuing, if often overlooked, major
problem in America. In 1977 almost one of every five people
living in rural areas (17 percent of the nation's population) was
designated as poor according to Social Security Administration
guidelines, as compared with one out of ten people (9.5 percent)
in urban areas. These 9.7 million rural poor are "surplus population," whose children often migrate to the cities. There they
tend to continue to live in poverty, while imposing additional
burdens on the already strained economy of the cities and depriving rural areas of their potential skills and leadership.

One innovative approach to rural poverty is the creation of
rural new towns and community land trusts. In an essay in
Resettling America: Energy, Ecology, and Community, Shimon
Gottschalk provides a comprehensive account of the philosophy
underlying the rural new towns concept.[11] Some of its major

ideological sources are the ideals of back-to-the-land movement proponent Ralph Borsodi, the Gandhian concept of alternative institutions, and the Israeli *moshav,* a modified version of the kibbutz. In applying the *moshav* concept of cooperative community to the rural South, proponents hope to make the rural new town an economic, social, cultural, and recreational hub for a larger geographic area.

New Communities Incorporated (NCI) was founded in Lee County, Georgia, in 1968 to develop a feasible alternative to impoverishment for economically marginal rural black American families. Organized as a land trust, NCI became the largest single-tract, black-owned farm in America. In 1980 its cooperatively owned (and heavily mortgaged) farm and wood lot covered 6,000 acres and provided livelihood for thirty-five families. The major crops are peanuts, corn, and garden vegetables. The group operates a roadside farmers' market, a day-care center, and a remedial education program. Allied with the Southwest Georgia Project, NCI also helps in the area's voter registration drives.

In 1982 the U.S. Civil Rights Commission issued a 196-page report featuring the alarming statistic that since 1920 almost 94 percent of the farms operated by blacks have been lost. The number of black-operated farms declined by 57 percent over a decade, two and one-half times the rate of loss for white-operated farms. Black family farmers will be virtually extinct by the end of the century if the current trend continues. The Civil Rights Commission report described the plight of black farmers as a "blight on the conscience of the nation." Despite their greater needs, black farmers had received only 2.5 percent of the total dollar amount loaned by the Farmers Home Administration farm credit program through 1981. To help rectify the situation and to ensure the very survival of black farming in America, the Civil Rights Commission recommended that specific federal action be taken to assist minority farmers.

For generations most rural blacks have been tenant farmers, squatters, sharecroppers, or hired day laborers working other people's land. For the first time those in the NCI project have their own land. The NCI has faced numerous crises but thus far has survived. Although the founding group is black, membership is open to all races, and the NCI wishes to live in fellowship with its white neighbors.

Gottschalk writes:

It may take a decade or two until a rural new town becomes economically self-sufficient. During its early years, it will require special financial inputs in the form of tax abatements, low-cost loans, grants-in-aid and special consideration in the location of public institutions. But such costs might be contrasted on a cost-benefit basis wih the expense of maintaining a large number of these families in poverty and on public assistance. The economic cost is calculable; the human cost is beyond calculation.[12]

The NCI project has coupled community self-help with outside expertise and financial resources. This support is vital until the local community can stand steadily on its own feet. Sensitivity is required of those providing external assistance; they must be helpful without being overdirective or patronizing.

The NCI received a good deal of assistance from the Institute for International Economics (IIE), an organization founded by Bob Swann and currently centered in Cambridge, Massachusetts. The IIE's Community Investment Fund has also helped people gain access to land and its productive resources by supporting projects in diverse areas such as Vermont, Appalachia, and Oregon. The Earth Bridge Land Trust in Vermont is composed of fourteen leaseholds in four different towns. The Appalachian land trust is envisaged as a model for combining small farmsteads with land conservation. Thus far the Oregon project provides access to land for a women's group, black sharecroppers, and migrant farm workers.[13]

This section has called attention to several innovative projects seeking to alleviate poverty and promote human dignity in rural America. These kinds of approaches to helping the underprivileged uplift themselves could be instructive to the United States and other nations in future assistance programs in Latin America, Asia, and Africa. About four-fifths of the world's people still live in rural areas, and far too many live in poverty. Creative ways have to be developed to help these people improve their lives, to give them reason for hope. This in turn would increase the possibility of nonviolent modes of social, economic, and political reconstruction in the poorer regions of the world.

Notes

1. Parts of this section were previously published in Arthur Stein, "Scott and Helen Nearing: A Tribute," *The Sun: A Magazine of Ideas,* no. 104 (July 1984): 28–33.

2. The Nearings' books include *Living the Good Life: How to Live Sanely and Safely in a Troubled World* (New York: Schocken, 1970); *The Making of a Radical* (New York: Harper and Row, 1972); and *Continuing the Good Life: Half a Century of Homesteading* (New York: Schocken, 1979). For a good recent article on the Nearings, their philosophy, and their life-style, see Ronald Kotzsch, "The Irrepressible Scott Nearing," *East-West Journal* (February 1981): 34–39.

The Nearings concluded *Continuing the Good Life* by recounting: "If we have helped a number of people to get started on a lifestyle more satisfying than that of the average United States citizen, they have in turn contributed measurably to the building of our own lives. . . . By the exchange of insights, experiences, and skills, they have cooperated as fellow workers in our joint efforts. We thank them and salute them as we continue in our own varied fields of productive and creative endeavor" (p. 184).

3. Cited by Jonathan von Ranson in "Wendell Berry: A Farmer Poet Resettling America," *New Roots: The Magazine of Energy, Community, and Self-Reliance,* no. 20 (New Year 1982): 16–20.

4. From Wendell Berry, "Family Work," in *The Gift of Good Land* (North Point Press, 1981).

5. George McRobie, *Small Is Possible* (New York: Harper and Row, 1981), 130.

6. "Beyond Price: The Story of H.O.M.E.," *Peacework,* no. 108 (May 1982): 12.

7. The name *Koinonia* is derived from a New Testament Greek word meaning togetherness. In 1942 a half dozen families began the community. Their goal was to introduce scientific farming methods into the area and, more important, to share their work and their wealth among themselves and bear witness as an integrated Christian community. One interesting anecdote is worth relating here:

As he sat one evening [in 1942] with the other members at the supper table, Clarence Jordan, Koinonia's founder, was called to the door by a small band of visitors, who promptly identified themselves as Sumter County Ku Klux

Klansmen and proclaimed: "We don't let the sun set on you people who eat with niggers." Clarence gazed out at the sun settling down behind the pines, then smiled, shook hands with the nearest of the men and declared, "I'm mighty proud to make the acquaintance of some folks who have control over the sun." Then he invited them to join the family for supper, but they turned without a word and stormed on back to town. (From William Hedgepeth and Dennis Stock, *The Alternative: Communal Life in New America* [New York: Macmillan, Collier, 1970], 176).

8. This program is described in *Rural Advocate* [a newsletter published in Charlotte, N.C., by the RAF and the National Sharecroppers Fund] (Spring/Summer 1980): 1–2.

9. *Rural Advocate* (Winter 1982): 4.

10. Information on the NSF's opposition to seed monopolies is drawn from various 1980–1982 issues of *Rural Advocate*.

11. Shimon S. Gottschalk, "Rural New Towns for America," in Gary J. Coates ed., *Resettling America: Energy, Ecology, and Community* (Andover, Mass.: Brick House, 1981), 161–181.

12. Ibid., 180.

13. McRobie, 133.

Chapter 3

Rebuilding Community

Cooperative Living

Together the words *communication, commitment, communion, cooperation,* and *common unity* combine to form a collage that describes the lifeblood of any vital community. They emphasize the qualities of sharing and respect, often spoken of but less often realized in practice. A dynamic community is composed of diverse individuals, each of whom is free to develop his or her unique inherent potential. We can have the individuality that is essential to the growth and maturation of each person without the divisiveness of extreme individualism.

Cooperative living does not necessarily mean living together in the same household or in some other collective arrangement, but it does involve being concerned for one another. It entails communication between people and an empathic feeling for the other's well-being.

We all know the pandemonium that can be caused by a major power blackout in an urban area, or by a heavy snowstorm that paralyzes traffic, affects public utilities, and hampers garbage collection. Yet most of us have experienced the helpfulness and concern people often show during such times. In Rhode Island people recall warmly the blizzard of 1978, which paralyzed the city of Providence and outlying areas for over a week. Coping with the snow made cooperative neighbors, at least temporarily, of some who had previously had scarcely any meaningful contact with one another. How welcome it would be if more of the concern and simple kindness engendered during crises could be carried over when things returned to normal.

Another example of people rising to the occasion of a crisis took place in Fort Wayne, Indiana, during the flood of 1982. Today's students are sometimes characterized as indifferent to their communities, but during the flood students and their teachers worked long hours making sandbags, building dikes, helping flooded-out citizens in shelters, and making food for workers. Half of the community's high-school students were involved, along with many teachers and other school personnel. A UPI photo of a "sandbag line" shoring up a leaky levee on the St. Joseph River was captioned, quoting the city's mayor: "The kids of Fort Wayne saved the city. There's no doubt about it."

In the United States in the 1970s there was an increase in land associations formed by families who wished to live in a peaceful rural setting, but lacked the finances to do so on their own. By pooling a portion of their resources they could purchase a sizable tract, keeping some acreage for individual homes and holding a large stretch of open land in common. Today's situation is far removed from the old frontier days, but ample opportunity remains to share and help one another.

Some people in urban or suburban areas are organizing neighborhood associations. Members may initiate projects such as shared gardens, in which they pool their resources to grow vegetables and flowers that everyone can use and enjoy. When people know one another better, an environment of greater safety and caring is created. This tends to protect the neighborhoods from criminal elements (crime rates are considerably lower in established neighborhoods) and decreases dependence on municipal police forces.

More cooperative households are also coming into being. Each household sets its own rules, according to the life-styles of its participants, and they pool such common responsibilities as child care, cooking, cleaning, and maintenance. By combining their efforts and financial resources, couples, single parents, and other single adults are able to obtain better living situations than they could afford on their own. Greater opportunities for companionship are also provided for both adults and children than many had had in narrowly defined nuclear families. Joint households are making use of large, old houses in urban areas that would be too expensive and impractical for any family or individual to own or rent. Thus far the trend toward cooperative apartment buildings and condominiums and the restoration of urban houses by joint households has been largely confined to the educated, mobile middle class. But there is no reason why more poorer people could not also benefit by these practices.

In the future more attention will have to be given to family relationships as well. Recent years have been marked by the decline of the nuclear family model of mother, father, Dick, Jane, and Spot portrayed in the primers of yesterday. Indeed the isolated suburban household headed by a father usually away at the office or golf course and including a housewife-mother who is literally "a wife of the house" and their alienated siblings has become subject to caricature. To paraphrase a Malvina Reynolds song, they all live in ticky-tacky little boxes that all look the same. It is no wonder such units are often breaking down. For one reason, the vocation of homemaker has been devalued in contemporary society. Many women understandably have rebelled against the advertising media's portrayal of the happy housewife getting her psychic satisfaction from maintaining glowing floors and eliminating rings around the collar. A number of men also are becoming uneasy with the strains and false values built into their truncated life-styles.

Women and men alike should have equal rights and opportunities to pursue their vocational interests, and within a family to share breadwinning and housekeeping responsibilities in ways appropriate to their situations. Both parents can take part in the nurturing of their children. Raising children in a loving and stable atmosphere can be very personally fulfilling and can be a boon to society as well. A happy home is the best place to build a child's character.

In both good times and hard times, encouraging and supporting one another is an integral part of a family way of life. In the best of traditional marriages, this was a constant source of strength, individually and collectively. A sound marriage or other close human relationship involves giving and forgiving, serving and encouraging one's helpmate or friend. Genuine affection and caring, engendered by a tender bond between mature human beings, is a precious gift.

And, although the nuclear family will undoubtedly remain the basic building block of our society, the support systems once provided by the extended family will have to be developed anew. Reconstituted extended families can also enjoy the rewarding times that traditional families have experienced—sharing chores, meals, and the trials and joys of life together.

American history has a long and often honored tradition of innovative experiments in intentional communities and communal living. These have been documented in Rosabeth Moss Kanter's *Commitment and Community* as well as other studies.[1]

Many of the much-publicized communal experiments of the late 1960s and early 1970s, although they met the needs of their members at the time, were by their very nature unstable and short-term. Some of today's communal groups, although less flamboyant, have developed greater stability and flexibility. They place more emphasis on practical cooperation and being sensitive to the needs of their individual members as well as to those of the group. Rather than maintaining indiscriminate "togetherness," they tend to be selectively cooperative in areas where the participants have a common interest in pooling resources. Conversely, they maintain more personal independence in matters where those involved prefer privacy or individual effort.

Ruth Montgomery calls attention to several 1960s and 1970s cults—most notably the Manson "family" and Jonestown—that cast a shadow over the communal movement.[2] When a group of followers allow themselves to be deprived of their free will and freedom of conscience by a charismatic leader, they are courting disaster.

By contrast, a healthy intentional community, collective, or commune is based on the principle of mutual self-respect and fairly shared responsibilities. Anyone should be free to withdraw at any time. The group should also be entitled to ask an individual to withdraw if he or she is not meeting his or her share of the responsibilities. There should be no coercion, overt or subtle. Leaders should be freely selected. One person may have originated the idea for the community and set it in motion and may thus have a vital and sustaining interest in its success. However, the respect or status accorded that person is not an entitlement for life; its basis needs to be maintained and renewed. A group is only as strong as the integrity, cohesion, and active participation of its members.

Finally, a few words should be said here about the importance of friendship in communities. Friendship is such a basic ingredient to the well-being of human community that we tend to take it for granted.

Friends are people we can open up to and feel comfortable with, and for whom we have special affection. The bonds of friendship can be enlarged to embrace those with whom we share interests. Our friendship circle includes those to whom we have given strong social support or who have provided such support for us. This support may extend from lending a helping hand to providing a sympathetic ear. A useful publication from the California Department of Mental Health emphasizes that "social support is the evidence that someone out there cares about you. It . . . is something that you naturally pass along or give in return for what you get. Social support works both ways."[3]

There is much evidence that social relationships have a profound influence on our mental and emotional well-being. Recent research also points to a correlation between the quality of a person's relationships with others and his and her physical well-being. In a depersonalized society that suffers from an increasingly overburdened and sometimes ineffective health-care system, community support systems based on friendship and mutual concern can be of considerable value. Development of milieus that facilitate friendships, mutual aid, and psychological support is essential to the overall rejuvenation of our society.

The New Citizen Movement

Those who decried the 1970s as a period of political inactivity should read Harry Boyte's *The Backyard Revolution: Understanding the New Citizen Movement*.[4] The book evolved from a project on the dangers posed by the social policies of large corporations. During his research and travels across the country in the late 1970s Boyte was surprised by the extent of resistance among aroused citizens to what he described as the "new corporate offensive." As he enlarged his inquiry, Boyte recognized that the wide range of community building, self-help, and cooperative efforts he found belied the negative labels with which some had summarily dismissed the 1970s. The grass-roots political activism he encountered and its potential for bringing about positive changes tempered Boyte's fears for America's future.

The major impetus of the new citizen movement came from the desire among a growing number of people to regain a sense of social and political empowerment in an environment that appeared increasingly indifferent to their needs and concerns. To this end many mutual-aid groups emerged, and the cooperative movement increased both in numbers and in the variety of people it touched. The revitalization of neighborhoods became a major concern. Strides were made by women organizing against sex discrimination, by workers seeking to combat occupational diseases, and by the elderly.

The citizen activism that emerged to confront the forces of "bigness" focused on concrete issues, such as bank redlining, unfair utility rates, and consumer ripoffs. Dealing with these issues has led to sometimes unexpected but very useful alliances— blacks and white ethnics, the young and the elderly, homeowners and welfare recipients have banded together to struggle against excessive corporate power and unresponsive government.

The Backyard Revolution documents the emergence, growth, problems, and possibilities of a plethora of organizations across the country, including the Citizens Action Program (Chicago), Communities Organized for Public Service (San Antonio), the Oakland (California) Community Organization, and Ralph Nader's Public Interest Research Groups. Much of the organizing theory for these groups stemmed from techniques originated by Saul Alinsky, but the unique needs of the 1970s also led to the development of new approaches, particularly in coalition building.[5]

Boyte is most encouraging when he cites examples of "ordinary people" developing a sense of purpose, self-confidence, and leadership capacity as an outgrowth of their involvement in citizen's organizations. In the 1970s a number of religious groups became more active sponsors of community organization. When church groups pooled their resources to promote social activism, alliances sometimes developed that crossed racial, income, and geographic lines. One successful example is the Oakland Community Organization (OCO), whose first organizational meeting in May 1977 was attended by a thousand neighborhood delegates. Boyte describes preparations for that founding meeting, which elected an elderly black man as its president, in some detail:

> The Catholic Church in Fruitvale, an Oakland neighborhood, filled rapidly. . . . People were clearly excited. Older white ladies exchanged polite good evenings with young black men. . . . On the walls of the church gym, names of different neighborhood units bore witness to Fruitvale's diversity: Fruitvale Improvement Association, Central Infantil De La Raza, Native American Youth Center, Neighbors in Action, and two dozen others. . . .
>
> When this meeting adjourned, many stayed to socialize and talk about how far the communities of Fruitvale had come since community organizing began. "Three years ago, we had a home two doors down that had rats running around it," said Margaret Hinkley, a Mexican-American woman who said her neighborhood group had changed her life. "That doesn't happen anymore in our neighborhood. I have seen change. I have seen my neighbors get excited. And I could see tonight that we're not just Fruitvale. After Saturday it's going to hit people that now we're all of Oakland.[6]

This kind of enlivening spirit fosters hope that, despite the tremendous problems facing our inner cities, people who resolve to work together can move their communities in positive directions.

In his enthusiasm for the new citizen activism Boyte acknowledges, but does not address as much as he might have, some of the problems of localism and narrowly defined self-interest stemming from America's past. For example, the 1890s Populist tradition, which he admires, had elements of racial and religious bigotry. And the 1970s saw local support and fund-raising for some rather seamy social and political causes.

Big is not always bad, nor is small necessarily beautiful, but I heartily agree with Boyte that our times call for reducing overgrown institutions to humanely manageable dimensions. In this sense, it is imperative to develop, in E. F. Schumacher's words, a new conception of "economics as if people really mattered." The unremitting systemic critique of corporate America in *The Backyard Revolution* may offend some political sensibilities, but it needs to be carefully considered.

Food Co-ops and the Cooperative Movement

Building cooperative organizations in which people voluntarily work together for mutually beneficial purposes is an important aspect of reconstituting community. During the early decades of the twentieth century, and especially during the Depression years of the 1930s, a wide variety of producer and consumer cooperatives were formed. But the advent of World War II, followed by the postwar return of economic prosperity and the McCarthy era of political repression, eliminated much of the interest and participation in the cooperative movement. However, by the late 1960s increasing societal ferment again led more Americans to seek out and affiliate with or create alternative economic institutions. Continuing through the 1970s there was a marked increase in consumer cooperatives, often located in small storefronts or basements, or in people's homes. They sprouted up in and around universities and also in local neighborhoods.

There are many forms of cooperative ventures, concerned with food production and distribution, transportation, housing, child care, and other activities. I will note here the most widely known and experienced form in the 1970s and 1980s—the consumer food co-op.

The available literature on cooperatives directly reflects the historical trends just outlined—in the 1930s a substantial number of books and articles were published, but from 1940 to the early

1970s very little was written on the subject. In preparing a work-study course on cooperatives first offered in 1975 at the University of Rhode Island, I sought materials that provided a sense of historical grounding and yet focused on the wide range of contemporary developments. Fortunately, a new outpouring of literature on cooperatives had just begun.[7]

According to the authors of the useful *Food Co-op Handbook,* cooperatives could be defined as "non-profit, democratically controlled groups of consumers that distribute high quality food, try to educate themselves . . . and seek to represent an alternative to the mainstream profit-oriented food industry."[8]

The first American cooperatives developed in the late 1800s along the lines of the Rochdale principles, which had originated among English weavers and farmers. Immigrant groups from Scandinavia also brought cooperative and populist ideals with them at the turn of the century. A consumer co-op founded by Finnish immigrants in Fitchburg, Massachusetts, in 1910 still exists, although it underwent substantial reorganization a few years ago. Large groups of immigrants to Minnesota also brought the nascent ideas of cooperativism, social democracy, and union representation from northern Europe. William Ronco, who has written extensively on food cooperatives, described the Minneapolis–St. Paul area in the 1970s as a "veritable co-op heaven," with more than ten cooperative stores, a warehouse, bakery, restaurant, trucking collective, and a dry goods/hardware store. With the resurgence of interest in co-ops, some young people of Scandinavian descent rediscovered their grandparents' zeal for cooperative institutions.[9]

Some of the cooperatives that developed during the 1930s are still functioning today. They generally sell their merchandise at prevailing market prices and return surplus profits to their memberships in the form of year-end rebates or dividends. The largest of these is the Consumer Cooperative in Berkeley, California, which in the mid-1970s had an estimated membership of 75,000 households and accounted for about 2.5 percent of retail food sales in the San Francisco Bay Area. In perhaps the largest concentration of co-ops on one block anywhere in the country, it has a co-operative supermarket, gas station and repair shop, hardware store, pharmacy, bookstore, taxi service, and natural foods emporium.[10]

The Berkeley food co-ops can compete on an equal footing with large-scale supermarkets. Also, like the other *Twin Pine* older co-ops, the Berkeley co-op has been a pioneer in consumer education, honest pricing and labeling, and child care for customers (practices long resisted by the commercial food industry). The co-op has been and continues to be a center for reformist social and political organizing and for neighborhood community meetings. Yet, ironically, in part because of its very business success, which enabled it to expand and develop professional management, members sometimes felt excluded from the co-op's decision-making processes. Partly as a reaction to this "bigness," a new wave of smaller-scaled co-ops grew up in Berkeley and San Francisco in the late 1960s and 1970s, starting with the "food conspiracies," that sought to remain responsive to the changing needs and wishes of their memberships. In the prevailing spirit of the times they reflected an "alternative life-style" look and emphasized participatory democracy.

It was partly as a reaction to the thought of food becoming an "industrial product" that many hundreds of co-ops sprouted forth in the 1970s. By that time control of the dominant food industry had reached frightening proportions. Many food-producing companies had been bought up by international conglomerates.

Tenneco, for example, owns gas pipelines, oil refineries, chemical plants and other heavy industries, in addition to Heggebladde-Marguleas, the country's largest marketer of fresh fruits and vegetables. Tenneco produces insecticides, fertilizers, and farm machinery, controls more than 70% of the U.S. date production as well as 10% of the table grapes, and owns a chunk of California agricultural land equal to twice the size of Rhode Island.[11]

As one student of agribusiness somewhat facetiously put it: "The Sunday dinner table today can be laden with turkey from Greyhound, ham from ITT, vegetable salad from Tenneco, potatoes from Boeing, pork chops from Ling-Temco-Vought, applesauce from American Brands, lettuce from Dow-Chemical, roast from John Hancock Insurance, strawberries from Purex and after-dinner almonds from Getty Oil."

Each person's view of cooperatives understandably reflects his or her own experiences, so I would like to recount a few of my own here. My initial participation in a cooperative was as a member of the Berkeley, California, Consumer Co-op in 1967–68. Returning to Kingston, Rhode Island, I joined a dozen other people in founding the Alternative Co-op in 1970. Starting as a weekly preorder co-op on a friend's back porch, it grew within a decade to about 250 members and moved to a permanent storefront setting in a basement at the University of Rhode Island renovated by members.

In general people start co-ops for one or more of these reasons: (1) to obtain better-quality products or services more cheaply; (2) to provide an alternative to existing product/service delivery systems and institutions, in other words, supermarkets; (3) to demonstrate that radical, new, or different ideas can work—for example, consensual decision making; and (4) to promote a cooperative way of life. The goals of the Alternative, as rearticulated in a co-op manual in 1981, are "to become involved in the process of providing whole foods (with as little packaging and processing as possible) at low prices—as an alternative to mass-processed foods of limited nutritional value. Members run the co-op, buying directly from wholesalers and local producers and providing all the necessary labor to keep the store well-stocked and operating smoothly."

As a nonprofit co-op the Alternative provides members with a wide variety of quality goods, cooking utensils, and the like. Whenever possible it acquires foodstuffs that are grown organically (without chemicals or pesticides). Food prices are kept down because the overhead is low. Members stock the shelves, record the prices, and bring their own bags and jars to carry home the unprocessed foods they buy in bulk. They do the purchasing and inventory and clean up the molasses or flour that may have spilled on the floor.

The experiences of working voluntarily together and sharing responsibilities are valuable in themselves. The skills necessary to organize and operate a co-op and build cooperative interpersonal relations are transferable to other aspects of our lives in a society that often lacks opportunities to develop such abilities. The Alternative is self-governing, based on the Rochdale principle of one person, one vote. Membership is open to all, regardless of race, religion, age, or sex. The egalitarian principles the co-op espouses provide an ongoing exercise in informed, participatory democracy.

The co-op is also a place where people can come together in a pleasant environment that they have created. It offers an appropriate setting for community-based activities and serves as an information exchange for social and political activities in the surrounding communities. Parents don't have to worry about their children grabbing candy at the checkout counter, and a children's play area is provided. Shoppers can also sit down in easy chairs and relax or talk with friends, browse in the member-donated library, or play the old piano that sits in one corner. Snacks, cups of herb tea, or freshly made spinach pie are also available.

The co-op focuses on consumer self-education—there is no commercial need to influence customers to buy products or to disguise ingredients or true price. Information is available on the sources and nutritional value of all products sold. The possibility of theft is also minimal; it would be like stealing from one's friends. Classes are offered on wok cookery, tofu making, tai chi, yoga, weaving, and alternative health care. The co-op is a place to pass out those extra zucchini grown in the home garden, distribute flower bulbs and cutting, and share recipes. Members can have the pleasure of grinding fresh, warm flour in the grain mill an hour before baking bread at home. And they can enjoy the scents of about a hundred herbs, spices, and teas, each in its large glass container, or buy homemade yogurt and Vermont cheddar at reasonable prices.

Alternative members take surplus food to a nearby home for the elderly, where they can discuss nutrition and health and swap stories with the residents. Members can also undertake a variety of other educational and creative outreach activities. Contact is maintained and collective buying done with other co-ops in Rhode Island and throughout New England.

Although this picture of the Alternative is extremely rosy, not everything goes so smoothly: From time to time the group has to rethink its organizational practices and recharge its batteries. Reaching a consensus on basic policy questions and other issues is sometimes a painstaking process. But the overall value accrued in respecting and listening carefully to a minority viewpoint—even a minority of one—benefits all. The consensual decision-making process is not always adhered to, but having it as a desired model serves the integrity of the co-op and its individual members well. The co-op naturally has its problems, but they are dealt with in good faith, and improvements often take place when members are facing and resolving the issues that arise.

Co-ops came in many varieties and sizes in the 1970s, from the 3,000-member Boston Food Co-op and the Madison Wisconsin Common Market (which fed 1,600 people) to smaller co-ops in Oxford, West Virginia; Laramie, Wyoming; Caribou, Maine; and Wolf Creek, Oregon.[12] During that decade food co-ops, like supermarket chains, began to move toward vertical integration. But they did so for the benefit of consumers, not corporate stockholders. Regional co-op federations, like the New England Federation of Co-ops, have set up contracts directly with farmer-producers. For example, a grower of relatively pesticide-free wheat fertilized with "green manures" in the Dakotas might be contracted to ship forty tons of wheat by railroad to NEFCO. The wheat would be warehoused and then distributed to dozens of co-ops in southern and central New England. By forging direct links with farmers and setting up their own mills, bakeries, and, when possible, transportation networks, co-op federations can distribute their food to local members at lower prices. A variety of "co-ops' co-ops" developed in the 1970s; they include NEP-COOP, the federation of Vermont co-ops; the Intra-Community Cooperative (ICC) in Madison, Wisconsin; Austin (Texas) Community Project; and Rochester (New York) Clear Eye Warehouse. One promising development in the 1980s has been the formation of Co-op America, which seeks to link producers and consumers in supportive, cooperative networks. Hundreds of groups offering a variety of goods and services from all over the country have joined this innovative movement to build an "alternative marketplace."

In 1972 Richard Margolis wrote an article in the *New Leader* in which he pointed out: "Cooperatism's history in this country has not been encouraging. After more than a century of struggle co-ops remain weak, marginal and in the eyes of many Americans, slightly far out."[13] Despite the increase in co-ops organized since then, the future of the movement today—over a decade later—remains unpredictable.

Co-op enthusiasts have to temper their optimistic visions of the future with a clearer understanding of the past difficulties and setbacks of the cooperative movement in America. Such an admonition was given in a short piece written in 1974:

> Do you know that in 1932 there were 6000 Cooperatives in Southern California, that Upton Sinclair was running for governor of the state on a Coop ticket. . . . What happened? Only four dozen Coops made it to the size of a storefront and the rest died within a few years because of volunteer burnout. Only three of their stores still exist. The rest went under in the post war boom when the capitalists could shift their money into supermarkets and McCarthyism was flourishing.
>
> There seems to be a tendency in the new food co-op movement to think of ourselves as totally unconnected with Andover, NECI, Fitchburg, Greenbelt, and the Co-op League of the U.S.A. Perhaps we have been frogs, sitting at the bottom of a well and thinking that circle of blue overhead is the whole sky.[14]

On balance, though, co-ops are more widely known and accepted and carry less of a "leftist" or nonconformist stigma today than at any other time in the post–World War II era. Also, increasing health consciousness and awareness of the importance of wholesome food in the general population reflect values shared with food co-ops. Historically, co-ops not only have been valuable for their own members, but have made a number of significant innovations later adapted by other institutions of society. The coming years may see an increasing variety of ways for people to join together to meet their basic needs and enrich their lives.

The Movement for a New Society

In the 1970s the Movement for a New Society (MNS) was one of relatively few groups that sought to combine sociopolitical activism with building cooperative community living situations.[15] The MNS began in the Philadelphia area in association with the Philadelphia Life Center; by 1980 it had developed a core of about 130 people living in twenty renovated houses in West Philadelphia. The movement also spread to other parts of the country and in the early 1980s had about thirty affiliated groups in America and links with nonviolent social change groups in India, Australia, the Netherlands, Britain, Japan, and several other countries.

The MNS began with people who were concerned about social justice issues and opposed to the American involvement in Vietnam. They envisaged their community as a "life-center," which would participate as an active force for social change in the neighborhood, the city, and the nation.

The movement defines itself as "a network of collectives working to bring about fundamental non-violent change." It holds that change in today's society must begin with the individual, through a reassessment of beliefs and a shift to a simpler, cooperative life-style. It calls for socio-change activists to come together and build structured mutual-support systems.

A number of the original MNS members came from Quaker backgrounds, although the humanistic rather than the religious aspects of that tradition most appealed to them. (Some still regularly attend Friends' Sunday meetings, but most feel philosophically attuned to the more secular orientation of the American Friends Service Committee.) The membership is quite diverse in education, occupation, and geographic background.

The West Philadelphia group started by collectively renting and renovating a number of old houses around Baltimore and Chester avenues. Later some of the houses were purchased. Together members were able to live in houses and with a life-style that none could individually afford. I visited the Philadelphia MNS in the mid-1970s during one of its monthly special weekends for potential members or supporters and other interested people. The weekends are organized by the outreach collective and provide opportunities to attend workshops, engage in discussion with members, and generally share in the life of the community.

The MNS houses appear well maintained. Each individual or couple has a private bedroom, and they share living, dining, kitchen, and work areas. By purchasing their food in common, sharing rents or mortgages, pooling transportation, and exchanging various skills and services among themselves, they are able to live on minimal average incomes. Although some MNS members hold full-time jobs like teaching, most adults work part-time and thus have sufficient free time for activities within their households and collectives and in the community. They can engage in political work or develop their own creative interests.

Most of the Philadelphia MNS households are composed of people between the ages of twenty and forty, but there are also some young children and a few vigorous older people, who might be called elderly in another setting. There are families with children, married and unmarried couples, and single people—each house decides which mix of people is best for it and who would be able to live most comfortably together. The cluster of MNS houses creates a neighborhood communal environment among people whose lives are moving in the same direction. They represent a variety of special interests, talents, temperaments, and life-styles—yet within this diversity exists a sense of common purpose.

The MNS strives to help its members break out of stereotypical roles. It holds that the collective consciousness of a group who work things through together can be more effective than that of a group in which individuals try to do everything on their own. In a supportive atmosphere it is easier to challenge oneself and be challenged by others to give up roles into which one has been socialized—whether they are based on sexist, racist, class, or ageist conditioning. Intracommunity workshops and support groups help facilitate this process. The MNS calls for equal sharing among men and women of maintenance tasks, cooking, cleaning, child care, bread baking, and breadwinning.

The MNS has also reached out to develop relationships with its neighbors. In the early 1970s its area of West Philadelphia was a deteriorating neighborhood in which many older people remained while the more socially or economically mobile younger people moved out. To help combat the street crime that is especially demoralizing for the elderly, the MNS called block meetings and helped organize a neighborhood association. One creative idea that emerged was to provide older people with Freon horns. If anyone witnessed a crime or a suspicious-looking situation or felt personally menaced, he or she could squeeze a horn, which emits a loud honking sound. Hearing the sound, other people would rush from their houses, also honking their horns. This and other means of building a watchful, caring community in the neighborhood soon substantially decreased crime rates.

The general form of decision making within the MNS is agreement through consensus. Using this principle, people tend to explore issues more carefully and to be sensitive to one another's feelings. Decisions reached this way are likely to be mutually satisfying. The MNS seeks to be egalitarian and noncentralist, like the society it wishes to build. Being democratic in structure, the organization recognizes that people with leadership ability are a valuable asset to the community, but that such ability does not bring with it any special privilege or honor. "Rather, each person is encouraged to self-development and self-exploration into her/his fullest potential." There is ample opportunity for community members to put forth their ideas and suggestions for group activities.

Much attention within the MNS is given to exploring the theory and practice of nonviolent social change. The interconnected problems confronting the contemporary world are discussed in macroanalysis study groups. Many MNS members participate in direct action projects that grow out of the study sessions, such as war-tax resistance.

The MNS study sessions encourage what sociologist Alvin Toffler has termed "anticipatory democracy"—people participating in drawing up a vision of a more humane social order. Espousing an egalitarian philosophy, the MNS hold that goods and services should be for social use rather than private profit. If this view were to prevail, the spread of income levels from rich to poor would be considerably reduced. Basic needs—food, clothing, shelter, medical care, education, public transport—would be guaranteed to all, for free or at little cost. The emphasis would be on improving the quality of life for the great majority.

Within the MNS communities, small collectives grow out of shared interest in particular issues. Six to twelve is generally considered an appropriate size for a collective. Each such group decides autonomously where to focus its efforts. In the Philadelphia MNS, for example, there are various political action groups, food co-ops, a recycling operation, gardening collectives, natural food catering, and a print shop.

As a broader, national organization the MNS sees room for a multiplicity of small economic and political groups, urban and rural, linked with one another when they have common concerns. Local and regional meetings not only conduct business but celebrate as well—they set aside time for sharing joy, sadness, music, food, and dancing and for strengthening the spirit of community.

The stated goals of the MNS are radical in the etymological sense of getting to the roots of society's problems. The organization sometimes gets a bit carried away in its use of rhetoric. Real revolution in our age involves not only systemic economic and political changes, but a complete "turning around" of the ways people view their own lives and relate to one another. To the extent that MNS members can actualize their commendable high ideals in everyday life situations, they can serve as role models for political activists in a society seeking to define its future.

Rural Community Experiments

The Federation of Egalitarian Communities is a group of intentional communities spread out over North America, ranging from homesteading groups to villagelike communities with similarities to the Israel kibbutz. They include Twin Oaks Community in Virginia, Aloe in North Carolina, East Wind and Sandhill in Missouri, Dandelion in Ontario, and Communidad Los Horcones in Mexico. Twin Oaks has existed since 1967; the others all began in the 1970s.[16] These experimental communities came together because of their common ideological beliefs and the wish to offer more people an alternative to an overly competitive and consumption-oriented society. They also share the aspiration of creating new concepts of society based on cooperation, nonviolence, and equality.

According to the federation, each of its participants: "(1) holds its land, labor, and other resources in common; (2) assumes responsibility for the needs of its members, distributing all resources equally or according to need; (3) practices non-violence; (4) uses a participatory form of government; (5) does not deny membership nor promote inequality among its members through discrimination on grounds of race, creed, age, sex, or social background; and (6) practices ecologically sound production and consumption."[17]

Each community enjoys a large degree of self-sufficiency through developing its own industries and growing and processing much of its own food. "They design and construct their own housing, and have built their own energy and waste recycling systems. They provide education for their children, as well as health care for all members." Federation communities are attempting to integrate the best of rural and urban life, providing their members with physical, emotional, and financial security. They experiment with new structures and constantly evaluate the extent to which they are meeting the needs of their members and living up to their professed goals.

In chapter 2 I first mentioned the rural new town concept in connection with the New Communities Incorporated project in southwest Georgia. Another rural new town, Cerro Gordo in Oregon, was conceived as a user-designed and user-financed community. New Communities Incorporated and Cerro Gordo represent two very different approaches to creating communities that will provide satisfying and sustainable living environments.

Chris Canfield, who since 1971 has been the director of the Cerro Gordo project, provides a good composite picture of the community as it has developed thus far.[18] Cerro Gordo was designed as an environmentally sound, human-scaled town for 2,500 people. It is located on a beautiful 1,200-acre tract of land about twenty-five miles south of Eugene. By 1980 around one hundred families were ready to begin building their homes amid the ever-green forest and meadows.

"A thousand acres are preserved for common use: fir and oak forests, meadows, agricultural land, a whole mountain on the lakeside, town greens and plazas and miles of track." Homes, community facilities, and businesses are being clustered in and near the village. Within the townsite people get around by bicycle, rather than private automobile, foot, and horseback; and there will be a community delivery service. Recycling programs will be organized by the community, and energy needs are fulfilled as much as possible by sun, wind, water, and biofuels. The community plans to be largely self-supporting, with jobs provided by education and publishing; community shops; small assembly and light manufacturing companies; an experimental college and growth center; writing, art, and crafts; and intensive agricultural production. This economic activity will support the services of the local bakers, doctors, shopkeepers, carpenters, and so on. It is believed that "the honesty inherent in a face-to-face community will replace the mutual exploitation often found in larger cities."

Homes and homesites are privately owned. All residents are members of the Cerro Gordo Cooperative, which sponsors community activities and facilitates democratic self-government and management of community land, utilities, facilities, and services. Every member takes an active role in shaping the community's direction—those who built the first houses took part in years of intensive planning before the first nails were driven. Adults will also take an active role in educating their children by participating in school programs and making the community itself an ongoing center of learning.

Cerro Gordo seeks to develop as an ecologically oriented village in harmony with its natural surroundings. Emphasis is also placed on developing a human-centered community—"we're striving to create a growth enhancing community that fosters a reintegration of the natural environment, the human community, and our inner selves."

Through the activities and publications of the Town Forum, prospective residents and others interested in the project can keep in touch with the latest developments.[19] Only time will tell how much the dream of Cerro Gordo will actually materialize and succeed in achieving its ideal.

In contrast with Cerro Gordo, which has carefully planned each step of its development, a community known as The Farm in Tennessee has had a more spontaneous growth. The experiences of its founder and driving force, Steve Gaskin, reflect the panorama of turmoil that swept over American society in the 1960s. Military service took him as a young man to Southeast Asia. There, amid the violence and confusion, Gaskin was introduced to what I will euphemistically call the mind-altering substances derived from local flora. He also developed an interest in the Buddhist and Taoist traditions of the region. Returning to the United States, he eventually became a graduate student at San Francisco State University and served as an assistant to the noted linguist Dr. S. I. Hayakawa. During the student upheavals in the late 1960s, Gaskin parted company with Hayakawa and became somewhat of a self-styled California guru. He soon gained a considerable following for his informal "Monday-Night Class" across the bay in Berkeley. During that time he developed a life philosophy that drew on widely varied sources.

Around 1970 Gaskin decided to tour the United States with a large group of friends, followers, and students. Together they refurbished and colorfully painted several dozen old school buses for their mobile living quarters. Many members of the caravan, like Gaskin himself, had been attracted to the San Francisco Bay Area in the 1960s. En route they stopped to visit family and friends, many of whom they had not seen in years. It was a time for fellowship, fun, healing, reconciliation, learning, and growth. Gaskin had developed considerable respect for some of the nation's traditions and urged his caravan companions to discover or rediscover what is truly good in America.

Looking for a permanent site to begin their own community, the group eventually purchased a large wooded property near Nashville, Tennessee, in 1971.[20] Within a decade The Farm's population grew to almost 1,500, but the numbers declined in the early 1980s because of internal economic difficulties and some disagreement over the community's future direction. Members of The Farm are vegetarians and grow much of their own food. Their major source of protein is soya, derived from the soybeans they grow. Soy products are also their major "cash crop." The Farm has adapted its own equipment for a soya processing plant, including a hydraulic press (for extracting soya milk) that had its origins in a toothpaste factory. The soya is used for bean curd (tofu), soya milk, and ice cream, a great favorite with the children.[21] The Farm also sells quality texturized soy products and nutritional yeast. All these are relatively inexpensive, and as more people become conscious of the relationship between nutrition and health, the market for the humble soybean and its derivatives is growing exponentially.

Some members of The Farm do various forms of contract work in nearby towns to bring additional funds into the community. The Farm also is involved in several outreach projects to serve its neighbors, including a health clinic staffed by doctors, nurses, and midwives. Some of The Farm women have studied midwifery and have revived and publicized this time-honored mode of assistance for home births. Another worthy project is Plenty, a foundation dedicated to providing nutritional food for the needy. A small group from The Farm went to Guatemala in 1974 to work in earthquake relief, and since then others have gone to that Central American country to participate in people-to-people assistance projects. Another small team went to Bangladesh to help set up a CB-radio communications system for a paramedical program.

The Farm has established itself as a religious community with Steve Gaskin as its head. It promotes a simple, nonviolent mode of living by its members. Except for the occasional use of native-grown marijuana for "sacramental' purposes, drugs have been eschewed by the community. Many members of The Farm, including its founder, used psychedelic drugs in the earlier California years, but in Tennessee they have learned to thrive more on the healthier, "natural highs" induced by good country living.

Stable family relationships are encouraged, and there is a loving appreciation of children. Members of The Farm have adopted babies from some mothers outside the community who would otherwise have aborted their unwanted pregnancies. Among the major community projects in the early 1980s is a self-built, solar-heated school for the several hundred children of the community.

The Farm seeks to be participatory and democratic in its governance. But in reality it has relied on the leadership, philosophy, and life-style preferences of Steve Gaskin. He and the community alike have had to be aware of the potential dangers of charismatic authority. As the years go by, however, The Farm appears to be moving toward its avowed goals of shared participation in the decision-making process.

Another intentional community that has a strong ecological consciousness is the Ananda Cooperative Village, which is located on a large tract of land in the mountains near Nevada City, California. Founded by Swami Kriyananda (born Donald Walters), Ananda integrates the discipline of Kriyayoga with the practical skills of community living and earning a livelihood. It offers a meditation and study center for visitors and operates a small alternative program that emphasizes experiential learning for high-school-age students from various parts of the country.

Innovative alternative energy projects can serve multiple purposes in a community, as in the case of the Cheyenne Community Solar Greenhouse in Wyoming. The project began in 1976 when fifteen low-income youths constructed three 16-by-20-foot solar greenhouses on vacant lots. The young people all were in trouble with the law and did the work as an alternative to jail. The original greenhouses are still in use and provide food for the community, including a group home for the elderly.

Spurred on by the program's success and its national recognition, Community Action of Laramie County launched another project—a much larger greenhouse. Writing in *Resettling America,* Gary Garber recounts how volunteers were involved "in all phases of the program, from planning and design to construction and operation."[22] These included high-school students, professionals, unemployed workers, and retired people. The 156-foot-long greenhouse was built in three sections to provide three different environments. By January 1978 crops were planted in the center section.

Looking at the overall value of the project Garber concludes: "The Community Solar Greenhouse means much to the people of Cheyenne. It is an alternative energy park where people can learn not only how to save energy but how to create it. It is a center where senior citizens can find meaningful work, and where young people can gain work experience and interact with older people. The greenhouse not only provides fresh food for Cheyenne's poor people; it is an information center and botanical garden where children can gain insight into their daily food." The Cheyenne experiment provides a model that other cities and towns could well emulate.

Urban Community Developments

Innovative developments in rural areas would alleviate some of the pressures on today's hard-pressed megalopolises. But for the present, millions of poor people are almost literally trapped in the nation's inner cities. In the economic downturn of the early 1980s many are unemployed or underemployed, uneducated, and immobile; they have little hope of improving their condition.

The older cities of the Northeast are still affected by the earlier shifts of capital to the Sunbelt, "white flight" to the suburbs, and the influx of black and Hispanic migrants. All these changes have put a severe strain on these cities' economies and ability to maintain even minimal services. Among the most visible signs of urban decay is the decline in roads, bridges, water and sewer systems, and mass transit. The Urban Institute in 1982 put the bill for repairing America's "infrastructure" at a frightening $572 billion.

A countertrend to these declines, which began in the mid-1970s, was the return of some whites to the inner cities. These were basically people who had tired of suburban living and wanted to be closer to their places of employment and the cultural aspects of urban living. Another major incentive was the lowered property costs in deteriorating neighborhoods. These newcomers have helped rehabilitate sections of cities such as San Francisco,

Philadelphia, Baltimore, and New York and have assisted the economic revitalization and "face-lifting" of downtown business districts.

Although a portion of the whites who have returned to the inner cities are well off financially and live an elegant life-style in high-rise condominiums, town houses, or refurbished apartments, the considerable majority are in the middle-income range. Some of those who can be considered urban homesteaders are also in the low-income bracket and are reclaiming abandoned or badly deteriorated buildings. Most of those returning to the cities are more open-minded about racial issues than the American population as a whole.

Yet problems grow out of the gentrification of these partially regenerated neighborhoods. Although most newcomers are not wealthy, as a group they are much better off financially than the racial and ethnic minorities, the elderly, the unemployed, and the relatively uneducated who have remained in the old neighborhoods. The influx of the new gentry leads to qualitative improvements, but, ironically, it then throws property values and rents out of kilter and makes housing unaffordable for the original residents.

The Over-the-Rhine sector of Cincinnati, Ohio, whose population in 1982 was about 60 percent black and 40 percent white, provides an example. The earlier inhabitants of the neighborhood, blacks and whites united in their poverty and frustration, have organized to make their voices heard, but at the time of this writing little had been done to ameliorate their condition.

In several encouraging instances the inner-city poor are participating in the planning and building or renovation of their own housing. Michael Freedberg in *Resettling America* cites one block in a Lower East Side neighborhood of Manhattan that in the 1970s made path-breaking strides in this direction.[23] Eleventh Street between Avenues A and B faced all the problems of urban decay. A number of buildings had been abandoned or set afire by arson, and some already had been totally demolished. But drawing on diverse resources, private and governmental, and primarily through its own "courage, commitment, motivation and plain hard work, a neighborhood once filled with despair [began] to show signs of hope."

The turnaround started when a group of block residents negotiated a loan from the city's Housing and Preservation Department to begin reconstructing a vacant, largely burnt-out building at 519 East Eleventh Street that the city had taken over through its tax-foreclosure program and scheduled for demolition. (Some of the fires in the building had been set by former tenants in protest against their slum landlord.) The agency was skeptical at first, but after a year of negotiations the loan was granted, and the reconstruction project began in 1974.

The building was purchased for a nominal fee with the understanding that its residents-to-be would provide "sweat equity"—their own labor—to replace the usual cash equity required by lending institutions. After eighteen months of work the building was ready for occupancy. The electrical, plumbing, and heating system repairs were done by the tenants themselves under professional supervision, as was most of the work required to replace the heavy, burnt-out structural beams. Thus a building slated for demolition was transformed into a nonprofit, cooperatively owned structure housing eleven low-income two- or three-bedroom apartments.

The tenants with some outside guidance installed solar and wind-based energy systems, the first of their kind in a low-income urban setting. They placed solar water-heating collectors and a wind generator (to supply electricity for the hallways and basement) on the roof. In addition they insulated and weatherproofed the building to cut down heat loss in the winter. During the first year tenants paid $2,600 for heating, compared with an estimated $7,000 for a comparable building without energy-conservation measures.

The new sense of community was further extended by conversion of an overgrown neighboring lot into a garden and a basketball court. The burnt beams from the tenement were used to make raised garden beds, which were most appropriate for the French intensive/biodynamic gardening methods that were adopted. Compost piles were built to enrich the poor soil. Growing their own fresh vegetables became a pleasant shared project and helped to increase participants' interest in improved nutrition. A community land trust composed of the gardeners and other neighborhood groups was set up, and this Trust for Public Land has helped create a precedent for community-based land groups elsewhere in the city.

Another creative addition was the building of a neighborhood playground, which involved the children themselves in planning and construction. Where possible, recycled materials gathered from the neighborhood were utilized.

Encouraged by the success of the "519" cooperative, two nearby buildings were soon being reconstructed under sweat equity principles. In these projects CETA job-training funds were utilized and sponsorship was provided by the new neighborhood-based housing group Interfaith Adopt-a-Building. Similar homesteading programs also have developed in deteriorating, low-income areas in East Harlem and Ocean Hill–Brownsville.

Of all the approaches tried to stem the tide of neighborhood disintegration in poverty-stricken areas of New York, the best results by far have been achieved where residents have been directly involved. Freedberg concludes that enabling tenants to become owners of their residences, especially on a nonprofit, cooperative basis, is a key factor to neighborhood rehabilitation. The principle of self-management also allows people a better opportunity to resolve the problems that burden their neighborhoods. Unfortunately, abandonments continue in the Lower East Side at a more rapid rate than neighborhood groups can rehabilitate. But to the extent that self-help redevelopment programs succeed, the entire city benefits.

The sweat equity idea soon spread to other cities. Through a (now discontinued) Department of Housing and Urban Development program, technical assistance was provided by the Urban Homesteading Assistance Board to projects in Boston and Springfield, Massachusetts, Chicago, Hartford, Cleveland, and Oakland.

The Stop Wasting Abandoned Property (SWAP) program of Providence, Rhode Island, is another instructive experiment in alleviating urban decay.[24] The organization was begun in 1975 as a nonprofit community group facilitating housing restorations by low-income and minority families. During its first three years SWAP helped new owners refurbish 175 houses. In a time of high interest rates and skyrocketing housing costs, a resourceful person could, with hard work and very little money, transform an abandoned structure into a livable home.

All SWAP's services are free. The organization maintains an updated list of available abandoned buildings. It offers to help prospective homesteaders find the "right house" to match their needs, skills, and financial situation. And after the house is acquired, SWAP assists with all the financial and construction details.

SWAP has molded a partnership of community, government, and private industry resources. The city of Providence in the initial years committed over $500,000 in grants and over $250,000 in 3 percent interest restoration loans for abandoned houses. Special legislation, initiated by SWAP and successfully lobbied for by its Homesteaders Cooperative, erases any back taxes on houses purchased through the program. SWAP's use of this unique legislation, as well as proper counseling to ensure that current taxes are not based on overassessments, has saved homesteaders considerable property taxes. The Homesteaders Co-op also utilized a government grant to establish a tool bank for its members' use. Nine banks and three credit unions are participating in a program that provides purchase/renovation mortgages for the houses. Incentive grants from the Mayor's Office of Community Development are considered the down payments for these loans.

SWAP's board of directors, formed in 1976, has thirty-five members, half of whom are homesteaders; the rest are community leaders and agency representatives. In the spring of 1982 there were five paid staff: a director, an assistant director/financial specialist, a bilingual counselor, a housing researcher, and a secretary. They were assisted by VISTA volunteers and CETA workers, and their funding helped by grants from the Mayor's Office of Community Development, the Rhode Island Foundation, the Urban Housing Corporation, and various churches.

SWAP's most important resources, however, are the homesteaders themselves. They are a mixed group: young and middle-aged, single and with families. Approximately one-third are black, one-third Hispanic, and one-third white. Most have little money, but they have two things in common—energy and skill. By doing their own work, they keep the cost of restoration down considerably. As of 1981 none of the loans they received had "soured." Each year SWAP organizes a free bus tour in which homesteaders open their houses to the public to show the results of hard work and cooperative initiative.

By pooling money, skills, and energy, SWAP has revitalized a substantial number of buildings with a minimum of red tape and administrative expense. SWAP functions on a modest budget, but it stands out among current public and private housing programs as one of the least expensive and most effective.

In the years ahead cities and towns will have to give more attention to rehabilitating old neighborhoods and helping low- and middle-income people obtain affordable housing. There is room for both private enterprise and a judicious combination of local, state, and federal governmental effort in this endeavor. Planning at all stages should involve input from those who are themselves living in the projects or neighborhoods.

Notes

1. Rosabeth Moss Kanter, *Commitment and Community: Communes and Utopias in Sociological Perspective* (Cambridge: Harvard University Press, 1972). Also see John Carr and Rosemary Taylor, *Coops, Communes and Collectives: Experiments in Social Change in the 1960s and 1970s* (New York: Pantheon, 1979).

2. The material in these two paragraphs is drawn in large part from Ruth Montgomery's discussion of charismatic communal leadership in *Strangers among Us* (New York: Fawcett, Crest, 1982).

3. *Friends Can Be Good Medicine* (Sacramento: California Department of Mental Health, 1981).

4. Harry Boyte, *The Backyard Revolution: Understanding the New Citizen Movement* (Philadelphia: Temple University Press, 1980). For a fuller discussion of the book, see Arthur Stein's review in the *American Political Science Review* (Fall 1981): 759–60.

5. Over several decades Saul Alinsky developed community organizing

into a highly skilled craft. His thoughts on the subject can be found in his two books, *Reveille for Radicals* (New York: Random House, 1969) and *Rules for Radicals* (New York: Random House, 1972). In the 1970s a dozen or so schools for community organizing developed around the country. Some of the highly skilled organizers and teachers of that period were Tom Gaudette, John Baumann, and, until his untimely death, George Wiley.

6. Boyte, 47.

7. Among the books I encourage students to read are classics such as Peter Kropotkin's *Mutual Aid* (1902), Martin Buber's *Paths in Utopia* (1949), and the writings of some of the early democratic socialists. Various publications and activities of the Cooperative League have maintained an important sense of continuity between the 1930s and the present; for example, Florence Parker's *The First 115 Years: A History of Distributive and Service Cooperatives in the U.S., 1829–1954* (1956) remains a definitive volume.

Two books published in the 1970s are also valuable: A. Dreyfuss, ed. *City Villages: The Cooperative Quest* (1973), and William Ronco, *Food Coops* (1974), with chapters ranging from "Coop History" to "How to Develop an Ongoing Coop Organization." *The New Harbinger: A Journal of the Cooperative Movement* (renamed *Co-op: The Harbinger of Economic Democracy* in 1979) and informational articles by the International Cooperative Alliance also contain helpful source materials.

In addition, we read E. F. Schumacher's *Small Is Beautiful: Economics As If People Mattered* (1973); *The Food Coop Handbook* (1975); *No Bosses Here* (1981); Susanne Gowan, *Moving towards a New Society* (1976); and Michael Schaat, *Cooperatives at the Crossroads* (1978). We also drew on publications such as *Communities Magazine, East-West Journal,* and materials from the Movement for a New Society and the North American Student Cooperative Organization.

For additional sources see Arthur Stein, "Cooperatives: An Alternative Institution," in *News: A Publication of the American Political Science Association,* no. 24 (Winter 1980): 1, 10–11.

8. *The Food Co-op Handbook* (Boston: Houghton Mifflin, 1975), 11.

9. William Ronco, *Food Coops* (Boston: Beacon Press, 1974), 6.

10. *The Food Co-op Handbook,* 27.

11. Ibid., 7.

12. Ibid., 32.

13. Richard Margolis, "Coming Together the Cooperative Way," *New Leader,* April 17, 1972. A student of co-op history, Margolis writes critically of some of the practices of the older *producer* co-ops:

Several white coops in the South have pointedly refused to sell fertilizer to their black counterparts; and on the West Coast some of the larger co-op grower associations, like Sunkist, have been charged with creating intolerable conditions for Mexican-American farmworkers.

Moreover, some co-ops have made a shambles of the Rochdale principles: they have closed their doors on new members . . . and in a few flagrant instances, have even scrapped the one man-one vote rule.

14. *NEFCO News* (July 1974).

15. Material for this section is drawn in large part from the "New Society Packet," a well-written compendium on the goals, structure, and activity of the organization published by the MNS Outreach Collective in Philadelphia. The collective also publishes *Dandelion,* which goes to supporters as well as members.

16. Twin Oaks almost foundered a few years after its inception but has since prospered and reached the optimal membership, about seventy people, for its limited acreage. Several of the Federation Communities have stemmed from the Twin Oaks overflow. Kathleen Kinkade gives an account of the early years in her *A Walden Two Experiment.* (New York: Morrow, 1974).

17. Quoted from a printout by the Friends of the Community, an association supporting egalitarian communities. The friends are people who share the aspirations of the communities but for the present have not participated in them "from the inside." The president of the friends is Dr. Joseph Blasi, who heads the Project on the Kibbutz and Collective Education at Harvard University.

18. Chris Canfield, "Cerro Gordo: Future Residents Organize to Plan and Build an Ecological Village Community," in Gary J. Coates, ed., *Resettling America: Energy, Ecology, and Community* (Andover, Mass.: Brick House, 1981), 186–213. Quotations in this section are from this essay.

19. Among the publications available from the Town Forum are *Cerro Gordo: Plans, Progress and Processes* and five other minibooks dealing with aspects of the project's first ten years. The *Cerro Gordo News,* a bimonthly newsletter, keeps the wide-support network for the community in touch with recent goings-on. The forum also organizes future residency programs.

20. Stephen Gaskin, *This Season's People* (Summertown, Tenn.: The Book Publishing Company, 1976), gives the founder's firsthand story of The Farm's first years.

21. George McRobie, *Small Is Possible* (New York: Harper and Row, 1981), 157–58.

22. Material in this section is from Gary M. Garber, "The Cheyenne Community Solar Greenhouse," in *Resettling America,* 350–365.

23. Material in this section is from Michael Freedberg, "Self-Help Housing and the Cities: Sweat Equity in New York City," in *Resettling America,* 263–81.

24. Basic information in this section is drawn from various leaflets published by SWAP and the article "S.W.A.P.: It Really Works," *Providence Journal Bulletin* (Sunday Magazine), October 29, 1978.

Chapter 4

People-Oriented
Economics and Politics

Appropriate Technologies

By the close of the Carter administration the American economy was beset by a twin spiral of economic stagnation and inflation, which were reciprocally linked to each other. To rectify this situation the incoming administration launched its antidote of "Reaganomics," considerably lowering inflation but increasing unemployment, which officially passed the 10 percent mark in September 1982. This statistic does not include the considerable number who were so discouraged that they had ceased even to look for work at the time, nor can it measure the human suffering and loss of self-esteem caused by such dislocations.

One of the approaches that could lead to a creative long-term resolution of the "stagflation"-unemployment cycle is that of E. F. Schumacher, who saw the need to develop appropriate technologies on a human scale. Schumacher's interest in both the theory and practical application of this concept led to his book *Small Is Beautiful: Economics As If People Mattered*. A man of diverse interests, Schumacher served as chairman of the British National Coal Board, cofounder of the Intermediate Technology Development Group, and a consultant on rural development in a number of countries. In addition to being a professor of economics, he also had working experience in journalism, business, and organic farming.

Schumacher dealt with the whole person. He was concerned about economic theory as it applied to the well-being of people. He maintained that economic development programs should be formed with this priority. His book *Good Work,* written with Peter Gillingham, discusses the importance of a person's livelihood to his or her morale and sense of self-worth. In his talks and writing he emphasized that each person, however menial or seemingly insignificant his or her occupation, should be accorded full human dignity. Also, much more attention should be given to creating alternatives to the mind- and spirit-dulling jobs often associated with the assembly-line production of the industrial era.

When Schumacher first put forth his ideas on simplifying technologies in the 1950s and 1960s, he was laughed at by many professional economists. Recognizing that Third World people could not solve their problems by imitating traditional Western modes of development, Schumacher and his friends Julian Porter and George McRobie organized the Intermediate Technological Development Group (ITDG) in Britain in 1965. This group helped create pilot projects in Asia, Africa, and Latin America.

The ITDG concluded that the less-developed countries had a pressing need for alternative modes of production scaled to locally available capital, labor, and skills. Utilized by small groups, these technologies could "make a significant contribution to the solution of the appalling social problems caused when human beings are denied the essential dignity of worthwhile work."[1]

In subsequent years Schumacher and his associates also worked with professionals from all walks of life who in the midst of seemingly monolithic structures sensed the need for reform. During the 1970s Schumacher became an influential spokesperson and role model among those in the United States and Canada looking for alternative approaches to economic development. In the 1970s counterparts to the ITDG were formed in Latin America, India, and Africa. Today alternative technology movements in the United States, Canada, and Britain are demonstrating that it is possible to create life-sustaining technologies which are low cost, sparing in the use of resources, and protective of the natural environment.

McRobie describes current projects as a drop in the bucket compared with what is needed to transform urban America on a large scale. To change from a consumer- to a conserver-oriented society involves a major shift in consciousness. There is obviously great resistance within the system to be overcome. Yet each new project is an encouragement to others and can stimulate additional initiatives.

Bill Smith, who lives in Jamestown, Rhode Island, exemplifies the spirit Schumacher sought to inculcate. After graduating from Harvard University, Smith acted on his Quaker principles and went to India as a Peace Corps volunteer. There he served in a village in Maharashtra as a diesel engineer mechanic. He learned the local language, lived simply, and established personal friendships.

Upon completing his Peace Corps stint, Smith returned to Rhode Island, where he is refurbishing an old farm with the help of several friends. He has made his land basically energy self-sufficient by building solar collectors and a windmill, which stores electricity in batteries. He has been a pioneer in working out an arrangement with the power company—with a little nudge from the courts on his behalf—to put the excess electricity he generates into the main power grid and take some back during periods of little wind. Smith has also been active in civic organizations and in peace-oriented groups such as the Mobilization for Survival.

Smith has gone back to his adopted village in India three times to follow up and renew the interests he developed earlier. The first trip was sponsored by Oxfam. On a shoestring budget he and the villagers constructed a direct-drive water-pumping windmill for a new irrigation project. Practically all the equipment was built by the people themselves utilizing simple technology and inexpensive, locally available materials that could be maintained by the villagers. He returned from his most recent visit in October 1984, having improved the irrigation project. This is person-to-person diplomacy at its best, and he has learned a great deal from as well as given of his skills to his Indian friends.

A number of groups in the United States are experimenting with human-scale technologies and their practical applications. Among these are the Center for Rural Affairs in Nebraska, Ecology Action in California, the Mountain Association for Community Economic Development based in Kentucky and Virginia, the Maine Organic Farmers and Growers Association, and the Rodale Press with its organic gardening and farm research center in Pennsylvania.[2]

One of the best known of these centers is the New Alchemy Institute (NAI) based on Cape Cod near East Falmouth, Massachusetts. The institute was founded in 1969 by John and Nancy Todd. John, Nancy, and Bill McLarney, a fellow researcher, had been studying fish depopulation in the Atlantic Ocean. They began to feel that their research was akin to being on a sinking ship and conducting a study of why people were running to the lifeboats. So they decided to put their scientific training to more relevant purposes. They brought together a group of young marine biologists, engineers, oceanographers, and agricultural specialists who were also interested in doing creative, environmentally oriented research.

The NAI seeks to utilize sun, wind, and water in ways that will allow people "to live lightly off the land." In their Cape Cod and Prince Edward Island centers they have developed experimental Arks, integrated systems that combine aquaculture (backyard fish farming) and hydroponics (growing plants without soil). Year-round aquaculture and agriculture take place in these passively solar-heated bioshelters. The whole system is virtually energy self-sufficient. In the solar-heated ponds fish and algae, both high-yield protein sources, are grown. Residue from the pond provides the nutrients for vegetables and fruits, which are also grown in the Ark. The water in the pond is constantly circulated by energy from a small windmill, and the moist, warm air inside the greenhouse provides an ideal setting for growing tree seedlings.

The Ark is designed as an experimental prototype for a commercial greenhouse. It is anticipated that such food production systems will be used to lower Cape Cod's dependence on outside food. The NAI experiments are also relevant to growing food in urban areas and more traditional rural settings. The institute is interested in sharing its work and has developed an extensive outreach program. Visitors are welcomed, and tours are provided each weekend from Easter to Labor Day. Each year a comprehensive volume of *The Book of the New Alchemist* is published to provide details of the ongoing work.[3]

Since the mid-1970s NAI has also maintained a center in Costa Rica. To involve itself further with Third World countries, in 1980 the institute founded a new organization, the Ocean Arts International.

During the 1970s there was a major leap in public awareness of alternative sources of energy. By the beginning of the 1980s growing interest in the subject had led to an increasing number of magazines and journals, such as *New Roots, The Northeast Sun, New Shelter, Solar Age Magazine, Renewable Energy News,* and *Doing It.* These highly readable publications feature accounts by people who are themselves "doing it," and sharing their findings and experiences with others. Solar energy lends itself to small-scale applications. Much of the innovative thinking and practical research in this area is being done by individuals and small groups who very often do not have access to outside funding.

Among the leading innovators who have restructured our understanding of energy and its relationship to technology is a Canadian, Amory Lovins. His wife, L. Hunter Lovins, hails from California and has a legal and forestry background. Together they form an outstanding team as educators and consultants on alternative energy.

In Amory Lovins's book, *Soft Energy Paths,* he points to the diversity, renewability, and relative simplicity of the "soft energy technologies."[4] A few examples include solar space heating, the use of wind for electricity or pumping of heat and water, photovoltaics, and conversion of farm and forestry residues to fuel alcohols. These forms of energy production offer advantages to nearly every constituency:

jobs for the unemployed, capital for business people . . . , savings for consumers, chances for small businesses to innovate and for big business to recycle itself, environmental protection for conservationists, better national security for the military, world order and equity for globalists, exciting technologies for the secular, a rebirth of spiritual values for the religious, radical reforms for the young, traditional virtues for the old, civil rights for liberals, local autonomy for conservatives.[5]

Obviously Lovins's enthusiasm has not yet carried the day; much resistance remains in the power structures to his way of thinking. Yet his "Here Comes the Sun" perspective points the way to a viable energy future.

Alternatives for Workers

The case for human-scaled enterprises merits careful consideration. Smallness in itself is not always a virtue and certainly is not a panacea to all socioeconomic problems, but "oversizeness" and depersonalization have run rampant in the institutions of modern society. Huge business and industrial enterprises are no longer synonymous with growth, efficiency, and innovative development. In fact, in 1980 approximately 80 percent of all new jobs in America were created by companies with one hundred or fewer employees.

A large number of working-class people are unable to cope with the imbalance caused by the rapid change in society and the dislocations it has created. The United States has no national "manpower" policy, and many of those who have lost their jobs have no means of "retooling" themselves. There have been few effective job retraining programs in this country since those provided by the successful GI Bills in the 1950s–1960s. It is interesting that West Germany has drawn on the example of those bills in establishing a national labor training system to lessen the impact of unemployment by teaching new skills to workers and assisting their relocation when necessary. A computerized system helps bring together available jobs and workers capable of filling them. Some form of comparable program in America could raise the morale of people who wish to work but cannot find gainful employment.

Whatever is done, the needs of the human beings involved

should be given prime consideration. Sociologist Theodore Roszak, in his insightful book *Person/Planet,* underscores the human right to "right livelihood."[6] He feels that the present urban-industrial culture is a dinosaur, which is "flirting with extinction." Yet the ideal of meaningful work has begun to reassert itself. Beginning on the fringes of mainstream society, more people are seeking to integrate earning a livelihood with their overall life values.

Roszak foresees greater demands for restructuring the working environment in clerical and assembly-line occupations, featuring more job sharing, mixed-skills teams, and "whole job" assignments. He also predicts increasing pressure for industrial democracy and more self-management in the workplace: "In smaller firms and newer industries we will hear about a new enlightened form of management which strives to take workers into responsible partnerships and even share the profits." Companies such as the Scott-Bader Commonwealth in England; International Group Plans of Washington, D.C.; and Bolivar Rearview Mirrors in Tennessee are providing present-day models for such management-worker cooperation.

A highly successful example of worker-owned industrial cooperatives can be found in the Basque region of northern Spain. The Mondragon movement, as this network of co-ops has come to be known, was founded in 1956 by Father José Maria Arizmondi, a resourceful village curate.[7] The project was instituted to help overcome poverty and unemployment in a region that still bore the scars of the Spanish Civil War and World War II.

The first Mondragon co-op, which manufactured cookstoves, incorporated the basic cooperative principle of one-person, one-vote. By mid-1982 eighty-five industrial co-ops had been set up, altogether employing well over 20,000 people. These co-ops produce refrigerators, washing machines and other domestic appliances, machine tools, and many other products. There has been only one failure in twenty-five years, a small fishing co-op. The industrial co-ops are associated with a flourishing consumers' cooperative, housing and agricultural co-ops, and other cooperative organizations that touch virtually all aspects of the workers' lives. Of considerable significance is support for all these enterprises from the cooperative bank, the Caja Laboral Popular, which is in turn owned and controlled by the workers' cooperatives.

A contingent from the Industrial Cooperative Association (ICA) based in Somerville, Massachusetts, visited Mondragon in July 1982 for an on-site study, especially of the entrepreneurial system used by the cooperative bank. The ICA describes itself as "a non-profit technical assistance organization that works with local employee and community groups to create worker cooperative enterprises."[8] It is developing further initiatives in the United States, based on Mondragon's success, for stable job creation on a regional basis.

Christopher Mackin of the ICA has noted that in recent years democratically owned and controlled cooperatives are being developed in the United States. To name a few, the Workers Owned Sewing Company of Windsor, North Carolina, employs fifty women, primarily black, in one of the poorest counties in the country. And in Burlington, Vermont, forty-five construction workers have organized themselves as a cooperative firm named Moose Creek Restoration.

It is encouraging to come into contact with business enterprises that combine an awareness of appropriate technology, a concern for energy conservation, a desire for cooperative employer-employee relationships, and a sense of old-fashioned integrity. Such a combination is found in the Vermont Castings Company (VCC), which builds efficient, finely crafted wood and coal stoves at its Franklin, Vermont, foundry.[9] Since the emergence of OPEC in 1973, the use of wood stoves has greatly increased among the energy conscious throughout the United States, especially in the colder climes. Along with solar, wind, and solid-fuel sources, wood provides an alternative to oil consumption. It is a boon for those seeking more self-reliance.

What helps make VCC so successful (in recent years it has become one of the largest manufacturers of wood stoves in America) is its attitude toward the public. Vermont Castings' customer-relations staff all have had some training in stove building and installation and are themselves users of the Defiant, Vigilant, Resolute, and Intrepid stoves they sell. They are available to answer questions not only during the buying transaction, but afterward as well. Their courtesy, honesty, knowledge, and genuine concern result in a strong bond of loyalty between company and customer. The staff answers many thousands of letters, and additional thousands of people visit the showroom. The company's attitude toward this service is expressed in the introduction to its 200-page illustrated reference book, *Book of Heat* (recently published by another Vermont company, Stephen Greene Press): "These people are our tutors. Their problems are the ones that need to be solved, their suggestions evaluated, their experiences shared. We at Vermont Castings are not the teachers so much as the students. In this book we have tried to distill and summarize our contacts with the wood and coal burners of America. It is our hope that with hundreds of thousands of tutors, we can't go wrong." Authorized dealers of VCC products are also encouraged to come to Vermont for mutual education and sharing of fun at an annual get-together.

There is a sense of family at VCC. As one close observer remarked, "The Company's president wears army fatigues and brings his dog to work . . . and the technical manager thinks the zucchini harvest is a proper occasion for a great celebration." Worker participation in decision making at every level contributes to good employer-employee relationships. The esprit and mutual caring among the staff is reflected in VCC's products.

The high morale at VCC was apparent during the third Annual Owners Outing, which the company hosted in 1981. Ten thousand friends from as far away as California and England gathered in Randolph to share a summer weekend of traditional entertainment and educational activities. There were tugs of war and lots of watermelon, demonstrations of pattern making and a tour of the foundry, a variety of workshops, lumberjack contests, and old-time fiddle music. The outing was another reminder that producing useful products and concern for people still make good sense in the sometimes cynical world of business.

Stirrings of Political Revitalization

The United States is known for its political stability and the resiliency of its two-party system. Historically it has been very difficult for new parties and political movements to gain a foothold in the American political mainstream. Often they have lost momentum when their most creative ideas were incorporated (or co-opted) at an opportune moment by the major parties. Nonetheless, civil libertarian, unionist, feminist, and antiwar movements and such "third parties" as the Populist, Progressive, and Socialist parties have been the source of many innovative ideas and have been focal points for political activism in their times. They have also been catalysts for socioeconomic and political change, and their contributions have broadened and enriched the democratic fabric of American life. Third parties and social change movements have also served as safety valves for expressions of dissenting opinion.[10]

In the 1960s cultural radicalism challenged the very fabric of American life. Recalling that period, activist-writer Marty Jezer notes that talk of imminent change was in the air among the New Left, especially after the 1968 Democratic Party National Convention in Chicago and the massive anti–Vietnam War protests: "In those heady circumstances electoral politics seemed outright reactionary, an attempt to channel a popular uprising into the status quo. On the left, only Michael Harrington and his (then tiny) band of democratic socialists tried to maintain a presence in the Democratic Party."[11]

In 1972 the McGovern campaign represented a temporary opening of the Democratic Party to the antiwar movement and more moderate elements of the New Left, but after Nixon's landslide victory, the party regulars soured on reform. The independent presidential candidacies in the 1970s of Dr. Benjamin Spock and Dick Gregory were well-intentioned, but left no ongoing organizations to build on. And attempts at forming new coalitions, such as Arthur Kinoy's proposed Mass Party of the People, quickly fell by the wayside. "The continued disorganization of the American left," Jezer maintains, "contributed to the right-wing victory of Ronald Reagan."

In this vacuum the prospects of the Democratic Socialists of America were revived and a new political party, the Citizens Party, came into being. These movements both recognized the importance of electoral and nonelectoral politics.

The Democratic Socialists of America (DSA) are attempting to leave behind the self-defeating divisiveness and ideological rigidity that has often hindered the American Left. The DSA was formed in 1981 through a merger of the Democratic Socialist Organizing Committee (DSOC) and the New American Movement. Each group brought a willingness to put aside past political quarrels and begin anew to find resolutions for the pressing problems facing society. Its initial combined membership of 6,500 made the DSA the largest democratic socialist organization in the country since the 1930s.

In the 1970s the DSOC had attempted to work with liberal elements in the Democratic Party to create a "Democratic Agenda." This was done with a certain ambivalence, for it was difficult to develop an independent socialist identity while being involved in Democratic Party politics. But the DSOC held that liberalism, despite its past achievements, "no longer responded to structural problems in the economy" and deemed it necessary "to take the battle for a 'New Beginning' into the Democratic Party." In the 1980s the DSA will probably maintain its earlier "ginger group" activity within the Democratic Party, but it will emphasize its own role as an alternative political and intellectual movement.

Use of the word *socialist* has often led to ambiguity and controversy. This stems in large part from its two distinct applications. One refers to the theory and practice of states that have had communist revolutions or takeovers—it refers to socialism already in existence and is used by proponents of the Soviet and Eastern-bloc national systems of political economy. The second usage, that put forth by the DSA and its democratic socialistic counterparts in Canada and Europe, harks back to the central core of the historic socialist tradition. It calls for maximizing democratic, participatory, and direct control over the social order by freely associating producer associations and for minimizing the bureaucratic and alienating aspects of state controls.

While recognizing that the word *socialism* is often a political liability in America because of its historic connotations, the DSA does not attempt to hide and indeed actively speaks of its commitment to the socialist concept. However, the party underscores in its credo that its ideals, like those of its social democratic counterparts in Europe, are democratically based: "We are Democratic socialists. The emphasis is on both words. We believe that democracy must be extended to America's economic system. Democracy is part of what socialism is. And we believe, equally strongly, that the changes we want must come about democratically."[12]

In its various statements on purposes, goals, and positions, the DSA envisages a humanistic society in which all people have a voice in the policy decisions that directly affect their lives—"a society where people are free to develop to their fullest potential, assured of individual liberties which safeguards against the dangers of an intrusive state."[13] The DSA respects the goals of blacks, Hispanics, Native Americans, and other minorities. It seeks to build a society that values cultural diversity and places a high priority on economic justice, to eradicate the sources of inequality, and on social justice, to change the attitudes that foster racism. It is working for the full equality of women and the elimination of sex roles that channel women into subordinate positions at home and at work. The DSA therefore supports movements in which minorities, working people, and feminists organize to protect their rights. It unites with those who are struggling for humane social services, a full-employment peace economy, and an educational system "that allows for individual fulfillment and for meeting the needs of an egalitarian and humane society." Utilizing coalition politics, the DSA wishes to build a mass movement to "eventually achieve full worker and community control of all economic decision-making." The party wishes not only to provide an incisive critique of Reaganomics or "politics as usual," but to put forth creative alternatives as well.

In the 1970s the DSOC was confined largely to the New York City area, to a lesser extent the San Francisco Bay region, and a number of college campuses. In the 1980s the DSA seeks to expand its geographic appeal and broaden the socioeconomic base of its membership to include more working-class people and minorities. It also wishes to dispel images held by critics—that it was primarily a debating society for academic socialist scholars and that it was too opportunistic in "cozying up" to Democratic liberals at convention time.

Numbered among the DSA's active membership at this time are author Michael Harrington; William Winpisinger, president of the International Association of Machinists; feminist writers and activists Gloria Steinem and Barbara Ehrenreich; U.S. Representative Ron Dellums; actor Ed Asner; Third World activist and Washington, D.C., councilmember Hilda Mason; writer Irving Howe; Santa Cruz, California, Mayor Mike Rotkin; New York City councilmember Ruth Messinger; and a substantial sprinkling of (mainly young) union, environmental, gay, feminist, student, peace, tenants' rights, and community activists. The DSA publishes a journal, *Democratic Left,* edited by Michael Harrington, which provides a lively forum.

The DSA is giving attention to its youth section, which initiated the Mobilization against the Draft in 1980 and has actively opposed U.S. intervention in El Salvador and Nicaragua. On college campuses it has supported union organizing drives, antiapartheid activity, and reproductive freedom of choice. The role of young people in the organization can be seen in the theme, "Reviving the Left," of the Conference of the DSA Youth Section held in New York City in December 1982.

The DSA is attempting to learn from and build on the strengths not only of the traditional Left, but of labor, civil rights, feminist, and community movements. It has also become far more receptive to people with religious convictions than have most other organizations on the Left. Activist theologian Michael Rivas has remarked: "Here I have found an organization deeply committed to both justice and freedom and willing to engage in the struggle for those ideals in an atmosphere of ideological pluralism."

Aside from DSA organizer Michael Harrington's personal background with *The Catholic Worker,* in recent years the ground for this congenial "atmosphere for ideological pluralism" in the DSA has been nurtured by the activist role of many Catholics in the popular opposition movements in Poland and Latin America and in the antinuclear and antiwar movements. More social consciousness and activism is emerging in Protestant and Jewish groups as well.

The Citizens Party (CiP) was formed in mid-1979 by a small group of liberals who were dissatisfied with the Carter presidency and felt that both the Republican and Democratic parties were too beholden to corporate business interests. The infant party sought to encompass a broad spectrum of support—from environmentally minded conservatives to nonviolent radicals who wanted to get to the roots of the nation's socioeconomic problems. Like the DSA, the CiP has very few blacks or other racial minorities among its members, but it also seeks more participation from those groups.

According to its party platform, the CiP "is dedicated to democracy at all levels of American life and to internal democracy within the Party itself, based on strong local chapters." Organizationally the party is in the populist tradition and seeks to develop from the grass-roots level up. It also decided to run candidates, whenever appropriate, for national office. At its founding convention in Cleveland in April 1980, the CiP nominated biologist-environmentalist Barry Commoner as its presidential candidate and LaDonna Harris, a Native American feminist and wife of former Oklahoma senator Fred Harris, for vice-president. At the convention the ticket was endorsed by notables such as author Studs Terkel, former U.S. Attorney General Ramsey Clark, and William Winpisinger. The CiP managed with considerable energy to get on the ballot in thirty states, more than any other new party in this century.

In November the party received 234,294 votes, a quarter of which were cast in California. Barry Commoner pointed out that the party's potential constituency was much larger than the presidential vote had indicated; CiP candidates for local offices in a number of states had received from 6 to 20 percent of the votes.[14] Several other factors detracted from the showing of the national ticket. A number of potential supporters voted for independent candidate John Anderson. Others, because of their concern about Republican Ronald Reagan, decided at the last moment to vote for Jimmy Carter. Wrangling within the CiP on how to run the campaign did not help either. Also, the party received little attention from the national media. Despite his frustration over the lack of publicity, Commoner remarked after the election that he was satisfied with the initial effort: "We have managed to show that it is possible to create an independent political party on the basis of an integrated set of ideas that are not handed down in some prepackaged political formula."

Taking its lead from Commoner, the party initially emphasized an anti–big business stance, but it has since softened this approach and focused on environmental and peace issues. Perhaps the CiP's major issue is ending the nuclear arms race and bringing about nuclear disarmament. Its platform supports the nuclear freeze campaign, political control of existing nuclear industries, and cuts in military spending. However, the CiP is not a single-issue party, as a number of third parties in American history have been. It puts forth a program advocating a variety of social, political, and economic reforms. It supports the restoration of a more healthful environment and calls for the rebuilding of the nation's cities, full civil rights for minorities and women, development of clean, renewable sources of energy, and movement toward full employment. The CiP is committed to the continuation of the free-enterprise system, but advocates more social controls on the powerful and more compassion for those who have not prospered.

In its initial electoral effort the CiP also put forth candidates in a number of congressional and local elections. In 1981, an "off-year," the party ran fifty-eight campaigns in fourteen states, winning a city council seat in Burlington, Vermont, and school board positions in Schenectady, New York, and Seattle, Washington.

Political historian and active CiP member Richard Walton commented that perhaps the most notable thing about the Citizens Party's second national convention in New York over the 1982 Memorial Day weekend was the simple fact that it took place: When the CiP was founded three years ago there was a lot of brave talk about that being the start of the continuing struggle to transform the principles on which the party was founded into an enduring and significant political force. But the history of the United States is strewn with the wreckage of short-lived political parties created by men and women no less sincere than we were.[15]

The convention was termed "a toddler with determination" by one commentator; its delegates "exuded a distinctly low-key, feet-on-the-ground, hard-at-work air."[16] Michele Puchard of California and Jim McClellan of Virginia were chosen as the new national cochairpersons. One of the highlights of the convention was the panel discussions with visiting members of sister "Green" parties from Britain, the Netherlands, West Germany, and Italy.

During the spring and fall of 1982, CiP candidates contested 114 local and statewide elections throughout the country. Candidates in Denver, Atlanta, Oregon, Washington State, and Vermont did quite well, winning between 15 and 47 percent of the votes cast. All told, from the 1980 presidential campaign through the end of 1982, the CiP entered 169 races in twenty-four states, and won 8.

One successful area for the development of grass-roots support has been Burlington, Vermont. In Vermont's largest "city" (population 40,000), the CiP won an additional two seats on the town council in the spring 1982 elections, giving the party a total of three people on the thirteen-member board. Coupled with the election a year earlier of socialistically inclined Mayor Bernard Sanders, a minority coalition of the three CiP members and two independents will try to implement a number of incremental changes. Their agenda includes tax reform, decentralization of community development decisions, worker participation in government management, and generally making local government more accessible to the people. To expand its support base, the CiP is striving to build a broader presence in surrounding counties and also plans to run candidates in upcoming House and Senate races.

Representative of CiP candidates during the 1982 fall elections was Hilary Salk, who ran for governor of Rhode Island. The CiP had just begun a state organization in Rhode Island, and Salk was its first candidate. Not only did she have creative ideas of her own, but she was willing to learn firsthand what was on other people's minds. Her background speaks of her interest in public service and people-oriented concerns. She was the founder of the Rhode Island Women's Health Collective and has worked in the Governor's Office as coordinator of the Children and Youth Services Project. She also taught high-school equivalence classes at the Urban Education Center. Salk's concern for a more peaceful world and nuclear weapons control is evidenced in her active work with Women for a Non-Nuclear Future and the nuclear freeze movement.

Salk was the only candidate in the governor's race to address openly the political "hot potato" of the Brown and Sharpe workers' strike; she called for an equitable resolution of the dispute beginning with the appointment by the governor of a neutral fact-finding board. She also called for the imposition of stiff penalties to bring about an end to the Ciba-Geigy Company's continuing pollution of the Pawtuxet River. Unlike those who believe that the importation of more high-tech industries will provide the main economic salvation for Rhode Island, Salk sounded a more cautious note. She also called for the development of appropriate-scale technologies that are environmentally sound. For example, Rhode Island is well situated to become a center for the development and production of wind and solar-based energy technologies.

The results of the election were predictable in a highly Democratic state, and the popular incumbent governor won handily. With little media attention or financial support, Salk polled only 2.1 percent of the vote. But her combination of idealism and practicality was a refreshing change from "politics as usual."

It would be foolhardy to predict what the future holds for movements like the Democratic Socialists of America and the Citizens Party. But their very existence and vitality during a lackluster period in mainstream politics is a source of hope.

Notes

1. From the Introduction to George McRobie, *Small Is Possible* by Verena Schumacher (New York: Harper and Row, 1981), xii.

2. See George McRobie, "A Guided Tour of Alternative Organizations in the USA," in *Small Is Possible*, 127–63.

3. Also see the brochure "Welcome to the New Alchemy Institute, 1982," (East Falmouth, Mass.: NAI, 1982).

4. Amory B. Lovins, *Soft Energy Paths: Toward a Durable Peace* (New York: Harper and Row, 1979), originally published by Ballinger for Friends of the Earth in 1977.

5. Amory B. Lovins, "Better to Take the Soft Option," in Mark Reader, ed., *Atom's Eve: Ending the Nuclear Age* (New York: McGraw-Hill, 1980), 138.

6. Theodore Roszak, *Person/Planet* (New York: Doubleday, Anchor, 1978). Quotations in these two paragraphs from Chapter 8, "Work: The Right to Right Livelihood," 205–40.

7. For discussions of Mondragon, see John Cort, "The Marvels of Mondragon," *Commonweal*, no. 370 (June 18, 1982); Robert Oakeshott, *The Case for Workers' Co-ops* (Boston: Routledge and Kegan Paul, 1978); and Alastair Campbell et al., *Worker Owners: The Mondragon Achievement* (London: Anglo-German Foundation, 1977).

8. From an ICA Report on the Cooperative Entrepreneurial System in Mondragon, Spain, October 18, 1982.

9. Information on Vermont Castings Company is in *The Book of Heat* (Brattleboro, Vt.: Stephen Greene, 1982), and the company's *Owners News*, a useful paper published several times each year in Randolph, Vermont.

10. The most recent book on the historical impact of third parties is Frank Smallwood, *The Other Candidates: Third Parties in Presidential Elections* (Hanover, N.H., and London: University Press of New England, 1983). Discussing the aftermath of the 1980 elections, Smallwood's final chapter focuses on "the two-party monopoly revisited" and "the future of third parties." The book also contains a detailed bibliography.

In his *Where Have All the Voters Gone?* (second ed., New York: W. W. Norton, 1982), Everett Ladd describes a growing dissatisfaction with the two major parties over the last few decades. He says that the resultant "dealignment" is leading to a breakdown of the old party coalitions and an interest in independent and third-party candidates.

Earlier writings on this subject include Norman Thomas, *Socialism Re-examined* (New York: W. W. Norton, 1963); and Daniel A. Mazmanian, *Third Parties in Presidential Elections* (Washington, D.C., The Brookings Institution, 1974).

11. Marty Jezer, a Citizens Party state committeeman from Vermont, is the author of *The Dark Ages: Life in the United States 1945–60* (Boston: South End Press, 1982). and "Electoral Politics and the Left: Why Activists Distrust It," *Citizens Voice* (the Citizens Party newspaper), vol. 1, no. 3 (November 1982): 10.

12. From the pamphlet "Democratic Socialists of America," published in 1982.

13. Information and quotations in this section are drawn from such DSA pamphlets as "DSA: The New Socialists" (New York, 1982), the party's monthly journal, *Democratic Left,* and the newsletter of the DSA Youth Section, *Days of Decision.*

14. This information and the quotation in the following paragraph are from a postelection interview with Barry Commoner by Frank Smallwood in *The Other Candidates,* 215–25.

15. Richard Walton, "Citizens Party Convention," *Citizens Voice* (November 1982): 1.

16. Jim Sleeper, "A Toddler with Determination," *In These Times* (June 16–29, 1982): 6.

Chapter 5

Active Nonviolence in the Nuclear Age

Nonviolence is the answer to the crucial political and moral questions of our time; . . . Man must evolve for all human conflict a method which rejects revenge, aggression and retaliation. The foundation of such a method is love.

Martin Luther King, Jr.

Finding alternative ways to resolve conflicts and to facilitate significant political and social change presents an ongoing challenge. And that challenge has become even more imperative in the nuclear age. In that context I will first provide some background on the concept of nonviolence and then discuss the role of active nonviolence in two 1970s demonstrations, one opposing the Vietnam War and one against nuclear weaponry. Finally, I will turn to the nuclear freeze campaign of the early 1980s and the longer-range goals of nuclear disarmament and limiting the production of nuclear energy.

Some Thoughts on Nonviolence

Historically, there are a number of sources for the concept of nonviolence, including Hindu, Buddhist, early Christian, and other spiritual traditions.[1] The term itself is an approximate translation of the Sanskrit word *ahimsa,* which suggests a reverence for all life. In its deepest sense *ahimsa* involves noninjury of others.

Nonviolence is not just a passive aversion to coercion and violence but an active pursuit of justice and humaneness in relations with others. Generally speaking, nonviolence is equally concerned with the goals and the means used to achieve them. Indeed, if the means employed to accomplish a desired end are not truthful and straightforward, they will inevitably distort the desired goals. Nonviolence also is linked to an overall philosophy of living. As Mohandas Gandhi once said, nonviolence is not like a garment that can be taken off and changed at will. I find it most fruitful to view nonviolence as an integral part of the search for truth, love, justice, and creativity in our lives. In today's endangered world ideas such as nonviolence can help the growth of a global-village consciousness in which all humankind recognizes our mutual interdependence. This is no longer just a utopian notion; it has become an increasingly practical requisite for a sane and survivable society.

Fundamentally, nonviolence is predicated on the recognition of freedom of conscience. This principle was well understood by Roger Williams and Anne Hutchinson, who helped make Rhode Island into one of the most religiously tolerant colonial settlements. Nonviolence also involves constant awareness of the dignity and humanity of others. The honorable treatment accorded the Indians by the Society of Friends (Quakers) during the leadership of William Penn illustrates this ideal. This principle has likewise been maintained by Friends and others who respect conscientious objectors' rights to refuse to bear arms.

A number of movements in recent American history have drawn on aspects of this philosophy, among them the antiwar, labor, and civil rights movements. Martin Luther King, Jr., Cesar Chavez, Dorothy Day, and others have attempted to understand what nonviolence entails and to incorporate it into their causes.

To some, a nonviolent approach to radical transformation of our society sounds "unrealistic" or "too idealistic." They may well ask: Is it not self-evident that right respects might? That war, conflict, and violence are intrinsic to human nature? Non-violent proponents seem spinners of an impossible dream.

Yet once something "impossible" has been done, it is no longer impossible. In the past forty years nonviolent campaigns have brought civil liberties to black Americans, given Mexican-American farm workers new rights and a sense of dignity, enabled poor Sicilians to overcome their fear and publicly defy the Mafia, opened the door to more equality for women, and united the people of India in a successful struggle for independence. These are only a few examples of effective nonviolent action. Strikes, boycotts, sit-ins, teach-ins, petitions, marches, demonstrations, refusal to pay unjust taxes, severance of diplomatic relations, and international embargoes are some forms of nonviolent action that have been used in many parts of the world. They have been employed principally in struggles for national liberation, human rights, better living conditions, disarmament, and fundamental changes in repressive political regimes.

There are, then, two closely related aspects of nonviolence. It has to do with the essence of a person's values and inner life and is reflected in daily activities. And it also is manifest in one's public participation as a member of society. A number of leading proponents of nonviolent approaches to social change hold that transformation of values must be rooted in the revitalization of community and in genuine communication between people. They see the confusion and discontent of "technological man" as stemming from a generalized alienation: estrangement from nature, one's inner self, and one's fellow beings.

Gandhian Principles and 1970s Political Protests

On several occasions Indian friends have asked me, What is the extent of Gandhian influence in contemporary America? This is a very difficult question to answer succinctly. First of all, I cannot talk in terms of *Gandhism,* because when one takes a vibrant life-force and reduces it into an -*ism* something vital is lost. Mohandas Gandhi himself once said: "There is no such thing as Gandhism and I do not want to leave any sect after me. I do not claim to have originated any new principle or doctrine. I have only tried in my own way to apply the eternal truths to our daily life and problems. . . . All I have done is to try experiments in truth on as vast a scale as I could."[2]

We know that Gandhi's living experiments with truth have had a real impact on many people's lives and thinking throughout the world. Yet we run into substantial difficulty when we attempt to quantify that influence. In this section I will approach one facet of the question—the range of Gandhi's "presence" in the nonviolent political activism, manifested by the protests against the Vietnam War and nuclear weaponry of the 1970s. We will review earlier manifestations of Gandhian influence in the civil rights and peace movements and then focus on two representative events. The first was Mayweek, 1971 in Washington, D.C., which featured the most widespread civil disobedience committed during the Vietnam War. The second was a demonstration in 1977 at the Trident nuclear submarine construction site in Groton, Connecticut.

During the civil rights movement of the 1960s, Martin Luther King, Jr., often spoke of Gandhi's considerable influence on his own intellectual-spiritual development and drew parallels between the Indian independence movement and the American Negro's historic struggle for social and political justice.[3] Application of the Gandhian principle of *satyagraha* (a Sanskrit word that means "holding on to the truth") were evidenced from 1955 to 1967 in black nonviolent resistance campaigns, which utilized marches, sit-ins, and boycotts along with community building and promoting the sense of dignity and self-worth of an oppressed people. Much of the impetus of this movement was halted, however, by Dr. King's assassination in 1968 and the simultaneous rise of the black power movement.

Also during the 1950s and 1960s, there was a small but committed nonviolent peace movement in the United States. Perhaps the most prominent spokesperson for the movement during these years, A. J. Muste, often mentioned Gandhi's profound influence on his life and his approach to conflict resolution.[4] Successful protests were launched against compulsory participation in civil defense air-raid drills in New York in 1955 and in other major cities. An extended campaign against above-ground testing of nuclear weapons paved the way for the Atmospheric Test Ban Treaty of 1963. Groups like the American Friends Service Committee, the Fellowship of Reconciliation, the Catholic Worker, the Community for Non-Violent Action, and the War Resisters League also initiated and took leading roles in the "Ban the Bomb" movement, the anti–Polaris submarine demonstrations, and various "walks for peace," such as San Francisco to Moscow in 1961 and Quebec to Washington to Guantánamo in 1963. The demonstrations conducted by these groups were disciplined and orderly. In the spirit of Gandhian protest, the municipal authorities were informed of the nature and timing of the actions, and civility was almost always shown to police and military personnel.

The first important demonstration against American participation in the Vietnam conflict took place in December 1964 when 1,500 people turned out in freezing weather for a rally in New York City. Other rallies were held soon after in San Francisco. By the end of the decade, the demonstrations grew much larger as discontent mounted against the ever-increasing escalation of the war.[5] In May 1970, for example, 100,000 people turned out for a hastily organized rally in Washington, D.C., to protest the Cambodian invasion. All sorts of tactics were developed to protest the war; they ranged from draft card burnings and tax resistance to various levels of confrontation with the civil authorities. (Several people committed themselves to extended fasts, but fasting does not capture public attention in America nor does it carry the moral suasion here that it does in India or Southeast Asia.) The war continued to grow, however, and with it the frustrations of those who opposed it. A split developed between those who were committed to principled nonviolent protest and those who were willing to countenance "any means necessary" to achieve the desired end.

It was in this uneasy atmosphere that the week-long demonstrations in the nation's capital at the beginning of May 1971 took place. A broad-based coalition organized this unprecedented event in which, for the first time, a large number of predominantly white, upper-middle-class Americans were willing to risk arrest and possible imprisonment for a cause in which they believed. Previously, in carefully planned civil disobedience actions of limited scope, demonstrators had courted arrest by sitting as witnesses for peace outside the White House and symbolically violating some minor ordinance. But there had never been an event involving direct, nonviolent action by thousands of people against the war. On the eve of May Day, about 20,000 people gathered in Washington, only a minority of whom had some previous understanding of *ahimsa* or *satyagraha*.

Complicating the matter for those who adhered to principled nonviolence were the varied approaches of the organizers, who came from a range of political backgrounds. Some either had a confused notion of Gandhi and *satyagraha* or did not care very much about the means they used to achieve their ends. Yet they recognized the power and appeal of Gandhi's name and drew up as the symbol for Mayweek a poster of "Gandhi with a Clenched Fist." The poster was supposed to symbolize unwavering resistance to unjust authority, but the fabricated image made those who had profound respect for the Mahatma and the integrity of his principles very uneasy. Some of these same organizers issued leaflets and talked about "closing down" Washington by blocking some of the key access bridges into the city, creating traffic jams in major intersections, and so on. Little of this actually took place, for the city police, unnerved by the possibilities and prodded by the Nixon administration, made preemptive arrests of many would-be demonstrators.

For several days before May Day, those who were committed to Gandhian principles sought to put forth their views. Black Southern Christian Leadership Conference volunteers including the Reverend Ralph Abernathy, a former co-worker with Martin Luther King, Jr., conducted workshops on nonviolent political action. Those who had thought of nonviolence only as a tactic to be used or discarded at leisure had an opportunity to learn of its potential for genuine personal and societal change. These veterans of Selma helped create a peaceable tenor in a situation that might have gotten out of hand. Their positive spirit was reflected in the words of Maris Cakars, a founding member of the magazine *Win: Peace and Freedom Through Non-Violent Action,* who wrote at the time:

Twelve thousand people were arrested with virtually no violence. That in itself is remarkable enough coming as it does after three years of "non-violence is dead." What's more remarkable is that in every instance of violence about to happen like "pig-baiting," etc.—there were people around to say "cool it," these are our brothers. For instance, there were some folks running around and pulling out the distributor caps of cars stalled in traffic. At the same time there were people from *Win* running after them trying to fix those cars.

The same kind of spirit prevailed in the jails where some people would try to cast the guards in the role of "pigs" while many others would fraternize with them and get them to the point where some contributed to the bail fund.[6]

Some of those who were committed to disciplined nonviolence avoided the disruptive activities in the streets on May 3, but participated in the more organized activities later in the week. They also utilized the time to contact legislators and establish communication with the poor and minority communities in the Washington area.

Thus, the disparate coalition of antiwar activists held together through the week. Successful rallies took place on the steps of the Capitol building; several members of Congress, including Representatives Ron Dellums and Bella Abzug, came forth to join the thousands of demonstrators.[7]

The specter of a large number of people gathered in Washington committed to risking arrest through civil disobedience apparently had a great psychological impact on President Nixon and his key advisers. In trying to defuse the movement they encouraged local authorities to break the law (for instance by making indiscriminate arrests in the streets and making mass arrests at peaceful rallies at the Pentagon and at the Congress). This in turn led to large-scale court actions exonerating almost every one of the approximately 13,500 who had been arrested through the week.

These events tended to convince the government that the American public might become uncontrollable and that large-scale civil disobedience would be likely if the war continued. Mayweek substantially increased President Nixon's fearfulness, which led to the events culminating in Watergate but also hastened his decision to get the United States out of Vietnam.

The withdrawal of U.S. forces from Vietnam in 1973 was soon followed by the collapse of the South Vietnamese regime. It also led to the disintegration of the broad-based coalition that had come together to oppose the war. By the mid-1970s America as a whole had again lapsed into a period of political quietism. But nonviolent activist groups such as the War Resisters League and the American Friends Service Committee continued their work. They focused on the ever-escalating American-Soviet arms race and, in particular, the proliferation of more destructive nuclear weapons and their delivery systems.

The Trident submarine is the ultimate weapons carrier in the nuclear arms race; it is capable of delivering over 400 nuclear warheads, each of which is far more devastating than the atomic bomb dropped on Hiroshima. Multi-billion-dollar contracts for the first five Trident subs were awarded to Electric Boat, a subsidiary of General Dynamics Corporation.

In April 1977 the Navy and Electric Boat had a keel-launching ceremony for the second Trident sub, named *The Michigan*. In turn, the Atlantic Life Community, a broad-based coalition of groups and individuals on the East Coast concerned about the Trident and ending the nuclear arms race, decided to respond with a people's keel laying in Groton on May 21 (Armed Forces Day) and the launching of a symbolic "Ship of Unmet Human Needs." Through newsletters and word of mouth, news of the demonstration was spread for three weeks. The theme of the day would be the affirmation of life and morality in opposition to the death and destructiveness of war graphically represented by the Trident.

A march was planned from New London to Groton, site of both the U.S. Naval Submarine Base and the Electric Boat Company. As many participants as possible were urged to arrive the night before in New London, where a general meeting and rally took place. An orientation and planning session was held in which the nonviolent nature of the march was emphasized. The participants made banners, watched films and theatrical presentations, and shared good food, music, prayer, and fellowship.

The next morning about 200 people assembled to begin the walk. The focal point of the procession was the "Trident Monster." It was dragon headed and 560 feet long—the exact length of a Trident—made of ropes and 12-foot-high bamboo poles held aloft at equal intervals by forty carriers. From the ropes hung 408 black streamers, symbolizing the twenty-four missiles carrying up to seventeen nuclear warheads apiece that each Trident will carry.

It was living theater. As the marchers trekked through the streets of New London, people came out of their homes and stores. Children ran after the procession, whose approach was heralded by a Scottish bagpipe and Japanese prayer drums. The drums had originally been brought to the United States for the Continental March for Peace and Disarmament, and their staccato beat was punctuated by the Japanese monks from Hiroshima solemnly repeating a mantric chant. Following the "Monster" was the "Ship of Unmet Human Needs"—a Trident replica in the form of a coffin. Then other marchers carried colorful banners and signs urging life over death. At the end of the long procession were musicians, singing antiwar and peace songs. Onlookers were given leaflets explaining why the marchers opposed the Trident. People could see that the demonstrators were friendly, and many smiled and waved.

The first stop was the New London Naval Underwater Systems Center, which designs the electronic systems and components for the nuclear weapons on the submarines. Then the marchers proceeded to the Naval Submarine Base, the largest of its kind in the world, and a site for nuclear weapon stockpiling. Needless to say, Groton would be one of the prime military targets in the country if nuclear war ever occurred. The demonstration was held in front of the entrance gates.

One of the highlights was a sobering talk by David McReynolds, a long-time activist with the War Resisters League. He spoke about the movements against war and forced conscription that had gone on since World War I and reminded his listeners that the struggle was a long and difficult one. The war machine has been built over many years, and it will take a long time to dismantle. He then spoke about the "ultimate deterrent strategy" involving the Trident and its Soviet equivalent.

Next came an act of symbolic resistance. Five people told the base authorities that they would like to enter the gates to plant a tree and some flowers, representative of life. Refused permission to do so, they walked toward the entrance with their plants and were arrested for trespassing. Then, in a dramatic gesture, four men and two women came forward with cups filled with their own blood and splattered it over the plaques which name chronologically all nuclear subs that have been built there over the years. (This kind of provocative action had started when the Catholic fathers Daniel and Philip Berrigan and their companions poured their blood on Vietnam draft files in Catonsville, Maryland.) The six then sat down in front of the bloodstained plaques, closed their eyes in prayer, and awaited arrest.

Following this, the trek continued on four miles to the site of the Electric Boat plant where the Tridents are being constructed. One of the talks given in front of the plant was by Marge Swann, a founder of the Community for Non-Violent Action. She spoke of the demonstrations in which she had participated over the years at Electric Boat and of her talks with people who worked there. She understood that the 15,000 people employed by the plant needed jobs, but if Trident and other war-related production were stopped or lessened, she noted, more constructive work might be created in the areas of housing, education, public transport, and health care. As important as the substance of her talk was her empathic tone. She did not try to make the workers feel guilty, but encouraged them if possible to seek other, more life-giving ways of earning a living.

Next, an Electric Boat representative was asked to permit flowers to be planted inside the front fence. When permission was denied a dozen people brought forth ladders and tried to climb the barbed-wire fence, but were quickly pulled off by the police and arrested. Only those who had planned to beforehand took part in this aspect of the rally. No one was pressured to join those who courted arrest by their symbolic nonviolent civil disobedience—there was a place in the demonstration for everyone. Although there was some tension during the arrests, the police conducted themselves well. Only one person who had been arrested appeared to have received rough handling. All those taken into police custody for the trespassing misdemeanors were released a few hours later.

The rally ended shortly thereafter. During the fifteen miles of the march, I had a chance to meet and talk with a number of people, including a Sister of Mercy from New London who teaches in ghetto schools, an Ivy League student who was "learning here what they didn't teach us in school," a number of people who had participated in the recent nonviolent demonstrations at the Seabrook, New Hampshire, nuclear power plant site, and a little black girl who walked many miles with us because she liked the "good vibes." As at Seabrook and in the antinuclear movement in general, almost everyone at Groton was white. One encouraging sign, though, was that the warmest reception from onlookers usually came when the march passed through predominantly black areas.

The self-discipline of the people who took part in the walk was impressive. One proviso was that all marchers should conduct themselves within the framework of nonviolent guidelines laid down beforehand. People were able to work together, and there was less evidence of personal egos vying for attention than was sometimes encountered during the Vietnam days. There were not different factions and individuals competing for the limelight or the speaker's podium, nor was there a sense of distinction between the leaders and the led. The walkers were courteous and respected the human dignity of the police and the military and civilian Trident personnel they encountered during the demonstrations.

During the Vietnam period activists were often so intent on opposing "the enemy out there" that they neglected their own lives and relationships and did not support one another. The emphasis in activism today includes building supportive and caring relationships with others. There is also a growing awareness that change starts from within. As Gandhi would put it, it is necessary to reform ourselves before trying to preach reform to others.

May Day 1971 was unique in that it was the only attempt during the Vietnam War to involve thousands of people in an action of massive civil disobedience. Indeed some of the participants sought to disrupt the functioning of the government itself. The Trident Walk, in turn, was representative of a good many smaller demonstrations held around the nation against nuclear weapons systems. The contrast between the way these two events unfolded indicates a reality of America in the 1970s—the number of people knowledgeable about and committed to nonviolent direct action in the spirit of Gandhian protest was limited. Large-scale actions meant the likelihood of departing from Gandhi's disciplined principles.

There were and are few in America who would identify themselves as Gandhians per se. Yet the influence of Gandhi was and is very widespread and has touched the thinking, politics, and lives of many who were most involved in the antiwar and anti–nuclear weapons campaigns. Perhaps more than any other twentieth-century public figure, Gandhi provides a common ground for those of diverse secular and religious backgrounds. His sources of inspiration were "as old as the hills" and are universal. The principle of *ahimsa* is enshrined in the living scriptures of a number of the world's religious traditions.[8]

Gandhi's approach has been adopted in the West by Martin Luther King, Jr., A. J. Muste, Daniel Dolci, Dorothy Day, Lanza delVasto, Cesar Chavez, Adolfo Pérez Esquivel, and many other creative women and men involved in movements for social change. They share a vision of the fundamental dignity, equality, and spiritual unity of all humankind.

Opposition to Nuclear Weapons

The 1960s and 1970s were marked by great public complacency and psychic numbness in America about the issue of nuclear weapons. Proponents of the status quo pointed out that the superpowers, following the Mutual Assured Destruction doctrine (with the appropriate acronym MAD) had not used their ultimate weapons in any "high-noon" showdown. In Europe, despite the heavily armed camps facing each other, an uneasy peace had prevailed. The rationality underlying MAD would undoubtedly continue to prevail in the future, it was argued, negating the possibility of nuclear conflict. During the Eisenhower presidency development of the "peaceful atom" had also helped improve the nuclear image.

After the Cuban Missile Crisis brought them to the brink of war in October 1962, the United States and the Soviet Union began talking more earnestly about arms control. An American-Soviet treaty banning nuclear tests in the atmosphere, in space, or underwater was signed in 1963, and a Nuclear Non-Proliferation Treaty in 1968. Four years later Chairman Brezhnev and President Nixon initialed the Strategic Arms Limitation Treaty, and SALT II was signed by the respective heads of state in 1979. Although SALT II was not ratified by the U.S. Senate after the Soviets intervened militarily in Afghanistan, its provisions have basically been respected.

But conditions worsened as the 1980s began. The Soviets placed new continental-range missiles in Eastern Europe. At the same time Ronald Reagan was elected president of the United States. Riding the backlash evoked by frustration over American policy failures in Vietnam and Iran and by the Soviet aggression in Afghanistan and the Polish situation, Reagan vowed to strengthen America's military forces. He aroused the electorate with promises to get tough with the Russians and to regain U.S. military superiority through a considerable buildup of both nuclear and conventional weaponry. The United States, he said, would not negotiate with the Soviets except from a position of strength. During his first year in office, President Reagan vigorously pursued this program. Domestic social programs were severely cut back and a record-high budget deficit was accepted to meet the high costs of the military expenditures.

In the autumn of 1981 several administration spokespeople and the president himself publicly implied that not only was a limited nuclear war in Europe conceivable, but it was winnable. The idea of a comprehensive national civil defense program that would enable American civilians to survive a nuclear attack was revived for the first time since the late 1950s. Some rather incredible statements were made in this regard, such as Undersecretary of Defense Jones's remark that all a person needed for survival in a nuclear attack was a shovel.

But all the talk about nuclear war being fought on their soil triggered widespread reaction throughout Europe, and major demonstrations took place from Bucharest to London. The nuclear arms question finally became a major public issue for the first time, initially in Europe and then in the United States. The threat of massive destruction was no longer an abstraction that might take place somewhere else; it had become a potential reality for Rome, Amsterdam, Boston, San Francisco—any hometown.

On May 19, 1981, George F. Kennan, America's former ambassador to Moscow, spoke out urging the United States and the USSR to begin negotiations immediately to reduce their present nuclear weapons stockpiles by 50 percent.[9] This proposal was especially noteworthy because Kennan had been the author of the Containment Doctrine, the cornerstone of American post–World War II efforts to block further Soviet expansion in Europe.

The Kennan proposal underscored how critical the next few years are—either a real breakthrough will be achieved while some flexibility remains in each country's defense planning, or both sides will be locked for many more years into building and deploying new weapons systems for their ever-elusive "security needs."

Another, perhaps more feasible way for the American-Soviet impasse to be broken also came to the public's attention around that time. It was embodied in the petition "A Call to Halt the Nuclear Arms Race," which urges the United States and the USSR to "immediately and jointly stop the nuclear arms race." Specifically, both nations are called to "adopt an immediate, mutual freeze on all future testing, production, and deployment of nuclear weapons and of missiles and new aircraft designed primarily to deliver nuclear weapons."

The horror of a possible nuclear holocaust is universally acknowledged. Yet over the next decade the USSR and the United States are estimated to be planning to build thousands of nuclear warheads to add to their present overkill capacity. Stopping the American-Soviet nuclear arms race is seen as a vital step in reducing the likelihood of nuclear war and preventing the spread of nuclear weapons to more countries. It is a prelude to creating conditions under which nuclear arsenals in all nations can be drastically reduced or eliminated.

Randall Forsberg, director of the Institute for Defense and Disarmament Studies and an initiator of the "Halt the Nuclear Arms Race" campaign, warned that we have only five years to implement the freeze before new weapons developments will make it unverifiable and, therefore, impractical. Within a year of Kennan's statement there was widespread support for the nuclear freeze campaign. By May 1982 endorsement had come from such varied sources as former SALT negotiator Paul Warnke, a number of retired generals and admirals, former CIA Director William Colby, 240 Catholic bishops, seventeen U.S. Senators, and 122 U.S. Representatives. Freeze resolutions were approved in Vermont at town meetings and by both houses of the state legislatures of six states—Massachusetts, Maine, Connecticut, Vermont, Oregon, and Minnesota.

Concerned professional groups such as the Physicians for Social Responsibility and the Union of Concerned Scientists through lectures, writings, and films made graphically clear in lay terms the medical realities of a nuclear conflagration. People from all sectors of the populace arose to register their protests. The Ground Zero Week held in cities and on college campuses throughout the land in April 1982 was especially effective in the awakening, and its related paperback quickly sold a quarter of a million copies. Jonathan Schell's eloquent *The Fate of the Earth,* which had been serialized by the *New Yorker* magazine, rapidly became a best-seller. A number of newspapers gave considerable coverage to the issue, including the *Christian Science Monitor,* which published an excellent five-part series on nuclear weapons in June.

The idea of polling voters on the freeze issue quickly spread. Referenda were placed on November 1982 ballots from Rhode

Island to President Reagan's home state of California. Church leaders spoke out as well. Catholic Bishop Leroy T. Matthieson in Amarillo, Texas, urged workers to give up their jobs in a local nuclear weapons assembly plant, and Archbishop Raymond Hunthausen, at the convention of the Pacific Northwest Synod of the Lutheran Church in Tacoma, Washington, called for withholding the portion of one's federal taxes used to support the military.

The June 12, 1982, march and rally in New York City on the occasion of the Second Special Session of the U.N. Disarmament Commission was probably the largest peace demonstration in American political history.[10] Estimates for the massive gathering in Central Park after the march passed the United Nations ranged from 550,000 to 800,000.

In southern Rhode Island, where I live, events relating to the march began on a Wednesday morning in mid-May, when a procession led by saffron-clad Buddhist monks from Hiroshima, Japan, walked through the streets of Narragansett and Wakefield. To the beat of their traditional prayer drums they chanted an ancient mantric plea for universal peace: "Na mu myo ho ren ge kyo." The marchers carried aloft the U.N. flag and a number of banners depicting the planet earth and the common brotherhood/sisterhood of all humanity. Having started in Maine in April, the walkers were headed for New York City.

Four similar processions began in Seattle, Los Angeles, New Orleans, and Montreal, all to converge in New York. These marches stemmed from a worldwide group of religious leaders and co-workers of many traditions—from Europe, Asia, Africa, Latin America, the United States, and the USSR—who first met in the spring of 1981 in Japan. Processions were organized in Japan and also in Europe. Three European march routes converged in Paris on Hiroshima Day, August 6, 1981. These walks for peace were a great encouragement to Europeans mobilizing against the nuclear threat and many thousands joined in.

Among those who had walked the entire way from Maine to New York City in the spring of 1982 were a mother carrying her infant child, Native Americans, and others from various walks of life. Each day the marchers were joined by local people who walked a distance with them. Food, rest stops, and overnight hospitality were also provided along the way.

A memorable event of the Narragansett-Wakefield portion of the walk took place when the marchers were joined by a sixth-grade class from the South Road Elementary School. The Japanese visitors were deeply moved by the children's presence. At a rest stop a letter the sixth graders had written collectively was read aloud and translated by a Japanese woman monk. The children had studied about Hiroshima and Nagasaki and expressed their hope that people would never again have to experience the horror of nuclear weapons.

Seventeen busloads of Rhode Islanders, organized by Women for a Non-Nuclear Future and the American Friends Service Committee, and many others in various conveyances, drove to New York City early on the morning of June 12. Ironically, the buses passed through impoverished areas of the South Bronx on the way to their parking area at Yankee Stadium. After seeing miles of often desolate urban landscape, the first prominent municipal building the group encountered was the massive Bronx House of Detention. Here was a graphic reminder of the grim reality for millions of young people growing up in an environment of urban decay. Appropriately, the dual themes of the rally were to end the nuclear arms race and simultaneously to focus attention on basic human needs. The resources consumed by the inflated military budgets of the world could be far better spent for education, job training, and community building.

A great variety of people took part in the rally and a buoyant spirit prevailed, even though many in the procession had to wait for hours in the crowded collage of humanity before their contingents began to march. Many young children were with their parents. In fact, throughout the preceding week a procession of children accompanied by adults had walked day and night outside the United Nations.

Virtually all segments of American and Canadian society were present in the march, and there were participants from every continent. A veritable alphabet of groups—Architects for Social Responsibility, Anthropologists for Peace, Business Executives for Nuclear Disarmament, Communicators for a Non-Nuclear World to name a few—were represented. Religious and women's groups were in abundance, as were union delegates. The Bread and Puppet Theatre from Vermont did improvisational theatrics, the Jugglers for a Friendlier World performed, and other such groups danced, chanted, or sang as they marched. Several somberly portrayed the plight of animals and plant life endangered by human despoilment of the environment. The dual themes of the march were expressed in placards bearing inscriptions such as "Mushrooms Are for Quiche, Not Clouds" and "Jobs, Education, Yes; Draft Registration, No."

The mood of the procession was uplifting, at times joyful, even though its basic message was very serious. The events were extremely well organized, and thousands of volunteers provided information for participants and assisted in crowd control. *No arrests* were made by the 15,000 police assigned that day, and their job was made much easier by the active cooperation of the demonstrators. There was even fraternization between some of the police and participants, especially during the rally-concert in Central Park; a few policemen and policewomen wore anti-nuclear buttons.

Virtually all the onlookers were friendly. In front of one department store several older women gave the V peace symbol and held up a sign saying, "We have to work today but we're with you in spirit." And from the sixth story of an apartment building two young men, one white the other black, waved from an open window. Below the window hung a banner reading "Black and White Together."

Hundreds of Japanese came to participate in the events, including some survivors of the 1945 atomic bomb attacks. Some had undergone untold suffering from horrifying conditions Torako Hironaka described in the book *Unforgettable Fire*. One group of about twenty Japanese musicians sat in a little pavilion outside the entrance to Central Park. Although most of their songs and chants were in Japanese, they established a bridge of communication with the onlookers. Their basic message was that the tragedies of Hiroshima and Nagasaki should never happen again, and that people everywhere should learn to live together in peace. Between groups of songs they showed interested people how to make little origami paper cranes, symbols of peace and good luck in Japan. Tears came to many eyes when everyone sang "We Shall Overcome." Citizens of two countries that had once been enemies now exchanged heartfelt expressions of goodwill.

Coretta Scott King told the audience, which overflowed Central Park's eighteen-acre Great Lawn, that "we have come here in numbers so large that the message must get through to the White House and Capitol Hill." Among the prominent speakers were Maggie Kuhn of the Gray Panthers, Dr. Helen Caldicott of Physicians for Social Responsibility, the Reverend William Sloane Coffin, and Bella Abzug. Also represented were several trade unions, organizations of the handicapped, and the National Association for Atomic Veterans, which is concerned with the welfare of war veterans now suffering from radiation-related diseases. Many of those speakers called for a new direction and purposefulness in the nation's political life.

Among the musicians who performed were Jackson Browne, who sang "For Every Man," Gary Bonds, Bruce Springsteen, James Taylor, and Linda Ronstadt. One of the highlights came when Joan Baez led the crowd in singing John Lennon's "Imagine." It was a moment to reflect on the potential of a humanity united in a quest for peace and social justice and to think of the similar gatherings taking place across the nation from San Francisco and Boise, Idaho, to Boston and Augusta, Maine.

A number of related events were sponsored by the religious community to underscore the themes of peace and arms control. A Sunday, May 30, service at the Riverside Church, featuring U.N. Center for Disarmament Director Jan Martenson. drew representatives from the United States, the USSR, and two dozen other countries. The program was part of the annual Peace Sabbath initiated in 1978 by the Reverend William Sloane Coffin, and around the world prayers for peace were offered in mosques, synagogues, churches, and pagodas.

On June 6 the newly formed Network of Light invited people throughout the world to pause for a few moments as part of a Global Day of Meditation and Prayer for Universal Peace and

World Unity. Those participating were encouraged to envisage their ideas of a peaceful earth.

Other events during the week of June 6–12 included a Mass for Peace and Justice at St. Patrick's Cathedral and a conference on reverence for life, which, inspired by Albert Schweitzer and Mohandas Gandhi, brought together representatives from Christian, Jewish, Buddhist, and other traditions. A private Jewish foundation, Emet ["truth"], sponsored a forum called "Facing the Peril of Nuclear War." And on June 11 the Religious Task Force of the Mobilization for Survival held an International Religious Convocation at the Episcopal Cathedral of St. John the Divine, where spiritual leaders of many traditions gathered to pray for a nuclear-free world. The participants marched to Central Park to plant a symbolic "tree of life" and then went on to the United Nations, where various groups took turns maintaining an all-night vigil. Appropriately, one interfaith service took place in a ghetto community on the theme of unmet human needs. During the U.N. Disarmament Committee sessions, religious groups joined a number of nongovernmental organizations in making presentations to the assembled national delegations.

To underscore their active, ongoing opposition to nuclear weaponry, about 1,700 men and women took part in a nonviolent "Blockade of the Bombmakers" on June 14. They offered themselves for arrest by sitting in the entranceway of the American, Soviet, British, French, and Chinese missions to the United Nations.

The question inevitably arises, To what extent were and are the governments of the 157 nations that took part in the U.N. Disarmament Conference affected by the worldwide outpouring of sentiment? There are, of course, no readily available answers. The speeches made by some of the heads of state at the conference were uninspiring, but others appeared visibly moved by the New York peace demonstration.

The conference ended with the General Assembly passing a set of resolutions that reaffirmed those adopted by the previous U.N. Disarmament Conference. No specific cuts in weaponry or deadlines were included. As one commentator wrote: "The superpowers don't want to be told how to deal with their strategic relationship, when and how to negotiate, and how many weapons to store in their arsenals. However, the governments of the major and medium powers do have to take the snowballing peace movement into account."

Widespread support continued to develop in the U.S. Senate for the Kennedy-Hatfield resolution advocating the nuclear freeze. And on June 23 the Foreign Affairs Committee of the House of Representatives by a 23–6 vote became the first congressional body to approve the freeze concept. This was despite the opposition of President Reagan, who stated that such a measure would lock the Soviets into a superior military position. Nonetheless, Reagan's call for the renewal of nuclear and conventional arms talks with the Soviet Union in the spring of 1982 indicated his administration's growing awareness of the widespread grass-roots support for an end to the nuclear weapons race. After a hiatus of three years, the strategic arms dialogue with the Soviet Union began anew in Geneva, Switzerland, when U.S. negotiator Edward Rowny shook hands with Soviet representative Viktor Karpov to begin the START talks. Both sides welcomed the renewal of talks, and it was hoped that something positive would emerge after the initial posturing and hard bargaining. In 1984, however, the United States, responding to Soviet installation of SS-20 in Eastern Europe, began its long-planned deployment of Cruise missiles in Western Europe. The Soviets then walked out of the Geneva negotiations.

A first major step toward halting the nuclear arms race would be to stop the production of any additional weapons and delivery systems. However, even if such an agreement is reached among the superpowers, further negotiations for dismantling the huge stockpiles now in existence would take years.

And even the elimination of nuclear weapons would have little effect on another critical problem—the worldwide proliferation of "conventional" weaponry, which has been rapidly increasing over the past decade. The major powers—the Soviet bloc, the United States, and the European NATO allies, have been the leading arms merchants in this buildup. As the Falkland Islands war recently demonstrated, today's conventional bombs are even "smarter" and more devastating than their predecessors.

Despite the almost unabated verbal hostilities between the United States and the USSR over the past thirty-five years, there has been no direct warfare between them. Over the same time frame, however, both have engaged in conventional wars in the "developing" world. Even where there is no direct involvement by the superpowers or their surrogates, conventional wars are increasing. During the early summer of 1982 alone, major conflicts were taking place in Iraq-Iran, Lebanon, Afghanistan, the Falkland Islands, southwest Asia, and several places in Africa. Civil strife was widespread in Latin America and elsewhere. In addition, the reports of Amnesty International documented political prisoners and major violations of human rights in scores of nations.

Both the United States and USSR continue to expand their stockpiles of chemical and biological weapons. The USSR has apparently used chemical weapons in Afghanistan, and its Vietnamese ally is reported to have employed them in Cambodia. Ironically, Vietnam itself was the victim of such warfare in the 1960s, when the United States deployed Agent Orange. (Among the most promising statements by the American and Soviet heads of state in mid-1982 were their declaration of willingness to negotiate a comprehensive treaty banning the future use of these weapons.)

In recent years there has been a steady erosion of the superpowers' capacities to dominate world events. Even if the East-West conflict were somehow resolved, the increasingly complex "North-South" situation would remain. Confrontations between the relatively developed and the underdeveloped nations, the economic haves and have-nots of the world are also possible.

New ways have to be found to understand and deal with these international problems. The challenges are great, and their resolution will require heightened awareness among the general populace and creative responses by their political representatives. The years ahead are fraught with obvious dangers, but they also present exciting possibilities for growth of understanding and positive changes.

The United States and the Soviet Union have long since reached the capacity for mutual overkill. The antinuclear movement does not intend to single out America. But this is where we live. The citizens of the United States, where there is much more freedom of speech and organization than in the repressive political climate of the USSR, can spark a constructive movement toward the abolition of nuclear weapons that could set a positive example for the Soviets and those living elsewhere in the world.

As Ervin Laszlo and Donald Keys, editors of *Disarmament: The Human Factor,* have put it, "before there can be disarmament there needs to be a significant change in our values and the way we view ourselves" as human beings.[11] Disarmament is not dependent on military and political considerations alone; its impetus must come from within the hearts and minds of all people. Protestations for peace will have little meaning if a transnational code of values based on the common unity of all people, is not developed.

Opposition to Nuclear Power

Related to the issue of the nuclear arms race is the growing concern over nuclear power. It would, therefore, be inappropriate to close this chapter without making brief mention of the opposition to the spread of nuclear power plants that grew in the 1970s.

In the 1950s–1960s government-endorsed arguments for widespread development of the "peaceful atom" dominated the public arena. The monopolistic forces controlling the budding industry presented atomic power as an inexpensive and inexhaustible source of energy for an unbounded future. Soon, however, voices of opposition, primarily from the grass roots, began to arise and could not be repressed.

The Three Mile Island crisis of 1979–80 finally brought the matter unavoidably into the public awareness. Nuclear technology has not provided the cheap, safe energy its advocates purported. Quite to the contrary, production costs have risen astronomically, and they are coupled with a variety of dangers, such as the invisible leakage of radiation.[12] The long half-life of radioactive materials extends their genetic dangers for many thousands of years. There is no demonstrably safe way to dispose permanently of the considerable quantities of radioactive nuclear wastes—an estimated 3 billion cubic feet—that already have accu-

mulated. Nor is there long-range protection against human error
and natural disaster. Even if we had permanent answers to the
technological and human problems involved, there is always the
possibility of nuclear plants and storage areas being affected by
geological or atmospheric disruptions. How do we guarantee
against hazardous materials being lost, misused, or accidentally
released into the human environment now or in the future?
Former plants will have to remain guarded for many years after
being decommissioned. Only a permanent authoritarian state
would have the capability to maintain long-term security, and
even that would not be effective without worldwide unanimity on
controls and sanctions. Such a scenario is frightening even to
contemplate.[13]

The splitting of the atom itself was a real technological
achievement, which culminated much scientific endeavor. Unfortunately, however, nuclear power was the outgrowth of the secret
Manhattan Project, which produced the atomic bomb in war-
time. Some of the scientists who had made the atomic bomb possible—including Einstein, Szilard, and Oppenheimer—later had
changes of mind when they saw the military monster that had
emerged and the scientific, industrial, and educational monolith
subsequently created to foster the nuclear power industry. After
the near-disaster at Three Mile Island, other, lesser-known nuclear engineers from several leading corporations resigned to
voice their opposition to the impending danger. A number of
former admirals and generals of the U.S. Armed Forces have also
been outspoken against nuclear weapons and power plants following their retirement.[14]

Nuclear weapons were created by the ravaging processes of
fusion and fission, essentially pushing together or pulling apart
the basic building block of nature itself. In the future, with an
expanded human awareness, nonviolent means may be developed
to draw energy from the natural flow of the atom. But there are
currently many soft-energy technologies that are far preferable to
anything the nuclear industry has developed. The control of
accurate information on nuclear matters and the dissemination
of misleading reassurances by politicians and the nuclear estab-

lishment must be vigorously addressed. The so-called ordinary person is capable of understanding atomic facts, despite the technicians' claims of scientific "privilege."

A major focal point of the growing movement against nuclear power in the late 1970s centered around Seabrook, New Hampshire.[15] Seabrook is a small seacoast town with lovely beaches and marshes thriving with bird life. In 1969 the Public Service Company of New Hampshire announced its plans to construct twin atomic reactors in the marshes. The townspeople were divided about whether the plants should be built. Local resistance was encouraged by the successful early 1970s struggle in the nearby town of Durham to block the massive oil refinery that shipping magnate Aristotle Onassis had sought to build. In March 1976, despite promises of tax benefits and more employment and business, the citizens of Seabrook voted against the plant 768–632 in a town meeting. Nonetheless, the public utility went ahead with its plans. By June 1976 opposition in Seabrook was joined by fifteen environmental and antinuclear groups from around New England to form an umbrella organization, the Clamshell Alliance. The Clamshell vowed to stop construction of the plant by nonviolent means. It faced formidable pronuclear opposition, including that of the powerful publisher of the nearby *Manchester Union Leader,* William Loeb, and his friend, Governor Meldrim Thomson.

After small initial actions, an estimated 2,000 Clamshellers entered the construction site on April 30, 1977, and were arrested. Their trials tied up the local courts for many months. This in itself became a major issue in an area that was becoming not only more antinuclear but also more concerned about the rising costs of trying and jailing so many demonstrators. Clamshell members themselves were organized in small, close-knit, regionally based affinity groups, and most used their time in jail for creative personal growth and shared movement building.

The largest "occupation" of Seabrook took place during the week of June 24–30, 1978. Clamshell vowed to occupy at least some of the Seabrook plant's 750 acres and to "install" some natural energy–producing equipment as a symbolic demonstration of its commitment to renewable forms of energy.

An agreement was reached with legal authorities and the Seabrook management to permit the Clamshell to enter a small portion of plant property. Six thousand "occupiers" then moved onto the site. According to Harvey Wasserman's recollections in *Energy War: Reports from the Front:* "Eighteen acres of bog, dump and wood lot soon erupted with tents, meeting centers, roadways, a "Bridge Over Troubled Waters," a first-aid tent, a makeshift stage, food stands, windmills, literature tables, T-shirt concessions, a geodesic dome, a solar oven, and various displays on conservation and recycling." Among those who took part were elements of the women's black, Native American, and environmental movements, all working together.

On Sunday an additional 12,000 people, many of them politically conservative local residents who had never attended a protest rally, came onto the site for a day of festivities and education. It was the largest assemblage staged by the American antinuclear movement up to that time. People of all ages and backgrounds were taking part; the fledgling movement had come of age.

Pete Seeger, Arlo Guthrie, John Hall, Jackson Browne, and others provided music that affirmed life as well as protested the "Nuke." A spirited new song by Charlie King of the Community for Non-Violent Action, appropriately named "Acres of Clams," provided an "anthem" for the Clamshell Alliance, and its resounding chorus echoed over the acres of temporarily reclaimed land. After the week ended the occupiers carefully cleaned up the site and left peacefully.

This exuberant demonstration did not, however, change the situation at Seabrook, and construction of the first reactor continued (despite the plants' owners increasing problems raising additional needed capital). The Clamshell Alliance itself was split the following year by disagreement over its future direction. But organic growth of a wide-scale antinuclear movement that encompassed a growing spectrum of the American and Canadian populace was underway, and the Seabrook Summer of 1978 had helped draw national attention to the cause.

Since the winter of 1977–78, the future for the nuclear industry has become increasingly cloudy. Mishaps in the accident-prone Millstone I plant in Connecticut and the Vermont Yankee plant led to temporary closings. Target dates for completion of several other plants were set back. Strong opposition developed against (and eventually defeated) the plant that the New England Power Company had planned for Charlestown, Rhode Island. Resistance mounted across the nation, from New England to Diablo Canyon in California.

From 1978 to 1983 there were no new orders anywhere in the United States for nuclear power plants. This, of course, does not minimize the dangers posed by the 150 or so nuclear plants already in operation or under construction. But, on the brighter side, only about 20 percent of the approximately 800 plants projected during the Nixon-Ford administration have been built or are underway. A combination of financial, political, and environmental factors have greatly slowed the once seemingly unstoppable momentum toward more nuclear power generation. As the cost of construction has escalated, it has become increasingly difficult to raise money for new plants. Lending institutions would simply rather put their resources elsewhere. Also, the earlier projections for America's energy needs have not been borne out because of conservation measures, the slowdown of the economy, and other factors. Despite the Reagan administration's pledge to help recharge the nuclear industry, it appears that, for the time being at least, the die is cast and very few new plants will be constructed.

But although the financial factor is important, especially in the recession of the early 1980s, we should not downplay the very significant role of the antinuclear movement in halting the spread of nuclear power in the United States. Professional groups like the Union of Concerned Scientists, local citizens' organizations, and demonstrators all have made considerable contributions. Their activism and emphasis on public education have also been decisive in prodding the Nuclear Regulatory Commission to perform its functions more effectively. Many dedicated women and men are giving of their time, energy, and resources to raise public consciousness about a vital issue. The nuclear versus natural renewable sources of energy debate goes beyond politics and economics; it touches on the need for a broad public reawakening and a reassessment of basic values and goals.

Notes

1. Part of this section was contained in Arthur Stein, "Non-Violence and American Political Protest in the 1970s," *Gandhi Marg* (the publication of the Gandhi Peace Foundation, New Delhi), vol. 3, no. 9 (December 1981): 529–38.

2. *Harijan*, (March 28, 1936). This paper was named for the "untouchables" of the Indian caste system, whom Gandhi called *harijans* ("children of God").

3. Martin Luther King, Jr., *Stride toward Freedom* (New York: Harper and Row, 1958). See also K. L. S. Roy, "Non-Violent Resistance in North America," *Gandhi Marg*, vol. 1, no. 9 (December 1979): 601–5.

For an in-depth study of the dynamics and potential of nonviolence as a force for social and political change, see Gene Sharp, *The Politics of Non-Violent Action*, 3 vols. (Boston: Porter Sargent, Extending Horizons Books, 1980); and *Social Power and Political Freedom* (Boston: Porter Sargent, 1980).

4. Gandhi's influence had already been felt in America for several decades. "His work in India was popularized in the United States by Richard Gregg, A. J. Muste, Jessie W. Hughan, Reinhold Neibuhr, and others; and by the 1940s pacifists had begun to implement American versions of Gandhi's programs. They started with communities, variously called colonies or ashrams, and by the end of the war, they had gained more experience with organized direct action techniques." Robert Cooney and Helen Michalowski, eds., *The Power of the People: Active Non-Violence in the United States* (Culver City, Calif.: Peace Press, 1977), 93.

5. See *The Power of the People* for a fuller treatment of these events.

6. Reprinted in *Win*, vol. 17, no. 10 (June 1, 1981): 10–11.

7. I recall speculating at the time:

Many people who could not relate to Mayweek may now be psychologically prepared to take a step beyond the usual demonstration or letters to their congressmen. What if even one-fifth of the half-million people who were in Washington on April 24th had, in a disciplined way, sat down as a group courting arrest in front of the White House, the Capitol or the Pentagon? How would the government react to 100,000 people including many "solid citizens" acting together in personal conscience in order to heighten the awareness of the rest of America about our Vietnam policy. . . . Such an action could hasten, once and for all, the end to our disastrous involvement in Indo-China.

Arthur Stein, "Mayday as Prototype?" *The Independent Man* (July 1971): 10.

8. For an excellent treatment of the links between Christian and Gandhian principles and insights see the chapter "From Gandhi to Christ" in James W. Douglass, *The Non-Violent Cross: A Theology of Peace and Revolution* (New York: Macmillan, 1966), 48–78.

9. Information in this section was drawn in part from the five-part *Christian Science Monitor* series beginning June 21, 1982. Other sources include the *New York Times, Jonathan Schell, The Fate of the Earth* (New York: Alfred A. Knopf, 1982); Ground Zero, *Nuclear War, What's in It for You?* (New York: Pocket, 1982); and the newsletters of the Union of Concerned Scientists.

10. Much of the content of this section is based on my personal observations. I also drew on the *Providence Journal* (June 12, 1982); *The New Paper and Peacework;* newsletters and leaflets of the Rhode Island Freeze Campaign, the American Friends Service Committee, Women for a Non-Nuclear Future, the Mobilization for Survival, and the June 12 Rally Committees; and broadcasts on National Public Radio's "All Things Considered."

11. From the introduction to Ervin Laszlo and Donald Keys, eds., *Disarmament: The Human Factor* (Elmsford, N.Y.: Pergamon, 1981).

12. Critical Mass, an antinuclear study group associated with Ralph Nader, compiled a "scorecard" for 1980 on each of the country's sixty-nine licensed reactors. Based on reports the power companies are required to file with the Nuclear Regulatory Commission, there were 3,804 reported incidents of equipment problems, design flaws, and human error, "ranging from relatively minor—such as improperly calibrated monitoring devices—to the very serious—such as leaks of thousands of gallons of radioactive coolant."

13. An observation by Mark Reader in *Atom's Eve: Ending the Nuclear Age* (New York: McGraw-Hill, 1980), 255.

14. For example, Rear Admiral Eugene Carroll was among the U.S. Navy's nuclear war planners before his retirement. On July 14, 1982, speaking before the representative town meeting in Groton, Connecticut, on the eve of a local nuclear freeze referendum, he explained why many of his friends in the military "agree that nuclear weapons can never be used to defend anything." Like many of his counterparts, he had held his profreeze beliefs before retirement, but had not been free to speak out. From an account in the *Providence Journal* (July 15, 1982): 1.

15. Information in this section is derived mainly from Harvey Wasserman's *Energy War: Reports from the Front* (Westport, Conn.: Lawrence Hill, 1979), 69–129, and from personal observations.

Chapter 6

Living More Simply and Serving Others

Voluntary Simplicity

Much of the violence and discord we witness throughout the world has its roots in dramatic disparities of material wealth. The day-to-day living patterns of the "haves" assume considerable importance. One encouraging trend in the 1970s was the growing number of people who voluntarily chose to simplify their lifestyles. The emphasis here is on the word *chose*. There is a great difference between freely deciding to live simply or being obliged to do so. Opting for a simpler life-style is far from living in grinding poverty, a condition in which too many people in the world are caught.

Living in voluntary poverty has been both a goal and a practice of many spiritual seekers and religious orders in varied cultures through the ages. The specific term *voluntary simplicity* was perhaps first used by Richard Gregg, a student of Mohandas Gandhi's philosophy, in 1936. To Gregg voluntary simplicity means "singleness of purpose, sincerity and honesty within, as well as avoidance of . . . many possessions irrelevant to the chief purpose of life. It means an ordering and guiding of our energy and our desires, a partial restraint in some directions in order to secure greater abundance of life in other directions."[1]

In his timely book *Voluntary Simplicity,* Duane Elgin draws on Gregg's descriptive phrase for his central theme. For Elgin the word *voluntary* connotes living "more deliberately, intentionally, purposefully." It involves being more aware of what we do, paying attention to our actions as we make our way through life. Simplifying precludes "making pretentious, distracting or unnecessary accumulations. It means being direct and honest in relationships of all kinds."[2]

Elgin in his work as a futurist–social scientist at the Stanford Research Institute had been investigating "grassroots experiments in more ecologically sound ways of living." He and his colleague Arnold Mitchell published their findings along with a questionnaire in a 1977 article in *Co-Evolution Quarterly* (a successor to Stewart Brand's *Whole Earth Catalog*). Readers of the quarterly included many who were experimenting with alternative life-styles. More than 650 people from varied backgrounds either responded to the questionnaire or wrote personal letters.

These respondents came from throughout the United States, Canada, and several European countries. They were for the most part highly educated (about 70 percent had completed college), and most had grown up in relatively well-to-do homes. Almost all were white, which is not surprising for "those whose childhood experience has been that of poverty are much less likely to become forerunners in choosing a way of life that they may perceive to be a perpetuation of that poverty."

Respondents had been involved with an alternative way of life for an average of six years, and the transformations they had undergone went beyond faddish and superficial changes in lifestyle. One young man from the Midwest expressed his hope that the interest in voluntary simplicity would not be trivialized by the media: "This is a country of media hype and VS is good copy. . . . The changes we're talking about are fundamental and take a long time. . . . If it is made into a movement it could burn itself out. I hope it spreads slowly. This way the changes will be more pervasive. Voluntary simplicity is the kind of thing that people need to discover for themselves."

Respondents tended to lower their levels of personal consumption and to acquire products that were "durable, easy to repair, non-pollutant in their manufacture and use, energy efficient, functional and aesthetic." They tended to move toward a healthier diet and foods that were more "natural, healthy, simple, and appropriate for sustaining the inhabitants of a small planet." They were inclined to join various cooperative ventures. They preferred "work that directly contributes to the well-being of the world and simultaneously allows one to more fully use his or her creative capacities in making that contribution." And they chose "smaller scale, more human-sized living and working environments that foster a sense of community, face-to-face contact, and mutual caring."

In many ways voluntary simplicity involves, to use the phrase of Buckminster Fuller, "doing more with less." The beauty of voluntary simplicity is that it is not an all-or-nothing proposition that has to take place overnight. People can move toward it at their own pace. The process can evolve over the course of a lifetime and can help the integration of the "inner and outer aspects" of a person's life.

A basic premise of voluntary simplicity is that how we live our lives can and does make a difference. Voluntary simplicity leads to more compassion because it involves conscious appreciation of the poverty of many people throughout the world. Many "reorientation" people have had the kind of economic and educational advantages that allowed them a wide range of choice in personal life-style. Yet they tend to opt for voluntary simplicity as they grow more aware of the implications of the fact that we Americans, who constitute only 6 percent of the world's population, consume over one-third of the world's goods and services.

By concentrating more on our spiritual side rather than focusing on material wants and needs, we could come to know ourselves better, have more significant relationships, and get our priorities in order. Simpler living can help facilitate efforts to establish a greater sense of community among people. It can help us avoid getting caught up in our day-to-day "personal worlds." Elgin concludes that small changes can become consequential, and that what he advocates is not a utopian dream but a "down-to-earth practical and realistic manner of living" that has already taken root in a number of Western nations.

It is significant that many of those who started to experiment with voluntary simplicity in the early 1970s did not do so as part of a social change movement. They were acting primarily on their own to bring their lives into a more harmonious balance with the needs of the rest of the world. Here lies a source of hope, for many of those moving toward simpler living come from the white majority community in America, which sets the pace for the country's consumption patterns and basically controls its economic and political structures.

Elgin does not mention those in the Western developed countries whose changes in life-style have occurred primarily out of economic necessity. For many of America's economic middle class who have felt the pinch of the recession, the necessary adjustments have been painful. But out of initial difficulties growth can also occur. Those who seek voluntary simplicity of their own volition and have incorporated it into their daily lives can provide role models for others who must make adjustments in their living standards.

Other recent books have developed similar themes on the efficacy and desirability of living simply and sensibly.[3] In her *Living More with Less*, Doris Janzen Longacre compiled a wealth of practical suggestions from the experiences of fellow Mennonites who have lived in all parts of the world.[4] Her book contains scores of personal accounts by individuals and families struggling to be free from the stifling affluence of modern society. Many of these Mennonites were engaged in teaching, community service, and church work. During their years abroad they had learned that people in the poorer, less-developed regions of the world have much to teach us about living, if we are receptive.

Longacre's earlier *More with Less Cookbook* is a boon for people who, in light of the world's food needs, want to select and prepare their food more responsibly. Among the other excellent cookbooks published in the 1970s is *Laurel's Kitchen,* in which Laurel Robertson and her Berkeley friends Carol Flinders and Bronwen Godfrey provide valuable suggestions and recipes for those making the transition to a vegetarian diet.[5]

Similar concerns motivated Frances Moore Lappe's widely read *Diet for a Small Planet* and its companion, *Recipes for a Small*

Planet.[6] These books document the points that not only do many Americans eat too much animal protein, to the detriment of their health, but by dining off the "top of the food chain" we are indirectly depriving others of basic grains and other vegetable-based proteins. Lappe's subsequent *Food First: Beyond the Myth of Scarcity,* coauthored with Joseph Collins, analyzes the origins of the world's present food problems and seeks to dispel the popular myths about why many millions of people are hungry or undernourished.[7] Lappe and Collins also are among the board members for the journal *Food Monitor,* published by World Hunger Year, which contains succinct analyses of food and agricultural issues throughout the world.

Those who have developed an awareness about the economics of food production and distribution are incorporating this knowledge into ther daily lives. Juanita and Wally Nelson are a couple who have consciously chosen voluntary simplicity as a life principle.[8] Getting up in years but growing younger in spirit, the Nelsons have made the vital connection between the practices of nonviolence and simple living. Born in a traditional black family in the Deep South, Wally Nelson was one of the first field workers for the Council of Racial Equality in the 1930s. Juanita first met him when she, as a journalist, interviewed him while he was serving a prison sentence as a conscientious objector. Together they have worked for human rights and peace in many ways.

In recent years they have been living on the grounds of Woolman Hill, formerly a Quaker life center, in northern Massachusetts. There they farm with hand tools, moving as much as possible toward a self-sustaining economy. In their three-quarters-of-an acre garden they grow about 75 percent of their food. They purchase their "real or imagined" remaining necessities with about $2,000 garnered annually from surplus vegetables from their garden, which they affectionately call the Bean Patch. Barter of goods and services also plays an important role in their economy and keeps them in contact with their neighbors. Occasionally they host workshops for visitors on such themes as "Non-Violence and Daily Living." Known by their friends as "the consciences of Franklin County," the Nelsons keep their house always open.

Visitors are welcome to join in their work, enjoy their infectious good humor, and imbibe some of their homegrown good sense.

In 1973 a group of Christian retreat center directors and their staffs convened at a restored Shaker village in Kentucky for their annual meeting. In the midst of conducting their business and enjoying one another's company, an unquenchable dialogue arose about how to relate personally to the problems of the world. Adam Daniel Finnerty, one of the conference participants, is a member of the Churchmouse Collective of the Philadelphia Life Center. He recounts in his book *No More Plastic Jesus: Global Justice and Christian Lifestyle:* "We may not all have been aware of the statistic that an estimated 15,000 people die every day in the world from malnutrition, but we were keenly aware that other people went hungry while we ate well."[9] In a subsequent meeting convened to discuss the issue further, a common pledge was drawn up. It was called the Shakertown Pledge "in honor of the original gathering place and because the Shaker community had believed wholeheartedly in lives of creative simplicity." The beginning of the nine-part pledge reads:

Recognizing that the earth and the fullness thereof is a gift from our gracious God, and that we are called to cherish, nurture, and provide loving stewardship for the earth's resources, and recognizing that life itself is a gift, and a call to responsibility, joy, and celebration, I make the following declarations:

1. I declare myself to be a world citizen.

2. I commit myself to lead an ecologically sound life.

3. I commit myself to lead a life of creative simplicity and to share my personal wealth with the world's poor.

4. I commit myself to join with others in the reshaping of institutions in order to bring about a more just global society in which all people have full access to the needed resources for their physical, emotional, intellectual, and spiritual growth.

Finnerty underscores that the pledge did not call for renunciation of material goods or for a life of poverty—"we don't want people to feel guilty every time they go to a movie or eat a box of popcorn." What was basically "new" and gave the pledge impact was "the firm declaration that personal piety, social conscience, and a simple lifestyle are all essential parts of a religious life that possess integrity."

Reaction to the pledge from clergy and laity alike was "swift and encouraging." "For many it was a formulation of a creed they had already adopted; for others it was a final impetus for lifestyle changes; for still others it was perhaps the first time they had been challenged to consider seriously a major change in their lifestyle."

The Shakertown Pledge marked a milestone in the movement toward simple and conscious living among a growing segment of the American populace.

Service to Others

Over the centuries there have always been people who have chosen to make service to others a central focus in their lives. Many of them are hidden from public view; others, like Mother Teresa or Dorothy Day, give us visible examples of the meaning of selfless service.

Dorothy Day started the first Catholic Worker House of Hospitality in the New York Bowery in 1933.[10] Rather than spend her time lamenting about the suffering of the poor, she voluntarily shared their poverty and worked for social justice. Until her passing at age eighty-three in 1980, Day's life was filled with the noise, dirt, and strife of the streets. Today there are perhaps forty Catholic Worker houses across the country. In Los Angeles about twenty volunteers run two hospitality houses, a newspaper, a soup line, a food co-op, and legal and medical clinics.

There is a need in our complex society for government to take a role in alleviating poverty. Yet the Catholic Worker philosophy is basically, "If you see someone who is hungry, you should feed him, not wait for the government to do it." Although Catholic Worker volunteers lack many material comforts, they receive compensation from the communal feelings they share at meetings and meals and the joy of helping people whom life seems to have written off. Their work provides an opportunity to put religious convictions into practice by serving rather than sermonizing. According to Jeff Gneuhs, a young Dominican priest who lives at the Mary House in New York: "The life is hard, but it doesn't have to be grim." It involves challenging work that helps the volunteers themselves to grow and develop their human potential.

Like the Catholic Workers, the Committee for Creative Non-Violence (CCNV) provides food and shelter for the hungry and homeless in Baltimore and Washington, D.C. Founded as a non-profit organization in the late 1970s, the CCNV is a vocal advocate for the indigent in the nation's capital. It provides a warm space for the many street people who have no other shelter on cold winter nights. Committee members collect food that otherwise might be thrown away. After much effort and picketing they have persuaded a number of large supermarkets to turn over surplus perishable goods at the end of each day for use in the CCNV free-food pantries. In August 1982 the group held a festive luncheon for 150 Washingtonians, including several members of Congress, of food scavenged from supermarkets' and wholesalers' dumpsters. The luncheon was organized to dramatize a House of Representatives resolution that would make it easier for charitable organizations and private groups to distribute America's considerable quantities of edible "waste foods" to the needy.

In the 1970s service-oriented groups ranged from Oxfam—with its programs of famine relief and low-cost, people-oriented developmental projects abroad—to the Hanuman Society, working with prison inmates. Those in Volunteers in Service to America (VISTA) and the Peace Corps assisted in many community-oriented projects at home and abroad. Participants in such programs have an opportunity to serve others and often gain valuable work experiences and cultural insights themselves.

I think it appropriate to end this section by calling attention to a service-oriented community in Tennessee that celebrated its fiftieth birthday in 1982. The Highlander Folk School, now known as the Highlander Research and Education Center, was founded in 1932 by Myles Horton in the mountains west of Chattanooga. Located in one of the poorest counties in the country, its basic purpose was to help those who were impoverished and exploited gain more control over their lives. Now in his late seventies, Horton recounted Highlander's history and educational philosophy in two extensive television interviews with Bill Moyers in 1981.[11]

Violating the prevailing Jim Crow–inspired laws, in the 1930s Horton invited whites and blacks to come together at Highlander for training programs in union organizing. The school, which in reality could be better called a life center, also soon became a principal gathering place for leaders and foot soldiers of the "long march of the southern blacks towards equality." Harassed by local and state authorities and by the Ku Klux Klan at various times, the center successfully resisted intimidation and continued its self-help programs.

Horton's wife, Zilphia, brought a strong interest in music to Highlander. Soon the school was helping, in Horton's words, "to cultivate the spirit and soul of Appalachia" and revive the region's cultural heritage through the creative use of drama, dance, and music. Zilphia Horton worked out a new, more singable arrangement of an old Negro hymn that had been picked up by striking tobacco workers in South Carolina and brought to Highlander. The song "We Shall Overcome" was sung for ten years at Highlander before it caught on and became the anthem of the civil rights movement.

The plight of sharecroppers and tenant farmers became Highlander's central focus in the 1970s. A landownership survey showed that three-fourths of the land in Appalachia was absentee owned. To deal with this and related problems, Highlander helped bring together about fifty regional organizations to form the Appalachian Alliance.

The Highlander Research and Education Center is now located on a farm near Knoxville and continues to use its resources for the benefit of the community. Myles Horton has given over his leadership position to younger colleagues, but still works "to make Highlander an instrument of empowering people, . . . to get people to understand that they can be creative and imaginative." Speaking of his approach to education, he told Moyers: "The way you educate is by example. You educate by your own life, what you are. I'm interested in people learning how to learn. Now, the only way I can help is to share my enthusiasm and my ability to learn myself. If I quit learning I can't share. I try to get people to feel, you know, be human." The struggle for social justice continues, but Myles Horton's life work demonstrates that "you can always have the hope, and sometimes the proof, that you can make headway."

Notes

1. Gregg's article, which originally appeared in the Indian journal *Viswa-Bharati Quarterly* in August 1936, was republished in *Co-Evolution Quarterly* (Summer 1977).

2. Duane Elgin, *Voluntary Simplicity* (New York: Bantam, 1982), 11. Quotations in this section are all from Elgin's book.

3. For instance, G. VandenBroeck, ed., *Less Is More: The Art of Voluntary Poverty* (New York: Harper and Row, 1978).

4. Doris Janzen Longacre, *Living More with Less* (Scottdale, Pa.: Herald Press, 1980). The author passed away shortly after the publication of this work.

5. Laurel Robertson, Carol Flinders, and Bronwen Godfrey, *Laurel's Kitchen: A Handbook for Vegetarian Cooking and Nutrition* (Berkeley: Nilgiri Press, 1976).

6. Frances Moore Lappe, *Diet for a Small Planet* (New York: Ballantine, 1975).

7. Frances Moore Lappe, and Joseph Collins, *Food First: Beyond the Myth of Scarcity* (New York: Ballantine, 1979). A comic-book version of *Food First*, which animates its basic theme for younger readers and underscores the importance of personal responsibility, was created by Leonard Rivas in the Educomics series. *Food First Comics* (San Francisco, 1982).

8. See Juanita Nelson's article "Bypassing the Buck," *New Roots* (Spring 1982): 24–27. Other information in these paragraphs is drawn from workshops given by the Nelsons and visits with them in Rhode Island and Woolman Hills, Massachusetts.

9. Quotations in this section are from Adam Daniel Finnerty, *No More Plastic Jesus: Global Justice and Christian Lifestyle* (Maryknoll, N.Y.: Orbis Books, 1977).

10. Information in this section is taken in part from the *Catholic Worker* newspaper (still a bargain at a penny an issue). The founding of the Catholic Worker by Dorothy Day and Peter Maurin is recounted

in Day's autobiographical *Loaves and Fishes* (New York: Harper and Row, 1963). For a recent study of Day's life and work see William Miller, *Dorothy Day: A Biography* (New York: Harper and Row, 1982).

11. See the transcripts of *Bill Moyers Journal*, "The Adventures of a Radical Hillbilly," WNET/Thirteen (New York: Educational Broadcasting Co.), Air dates June 5 and 11, 1981, from which quotations in this section are taken.

Chapter 7

The Quest for Transformation

In his *Revolution of Hope,* published in 1968, Erich Fromm envisaged the development of a broad-based movement beginning in America in which the goal of significant social change would be nurtured with new spiritual perspectives.[1] Such a movement would be open to people of all ages and backgrounds, conservatives and radicals, who were searching for new directions. Fromm felt that its moving force would be committed members who would work together in small groups toward personal changes, and in the process demonstrate "the strengths and joys of people who have deep convictions without being fanatical . . . and who are imaginative without being unrealistic." The movement could help humanize an overly technological and compartmentalized society, and within twenty years could be a major catalyst for substantial change, not only in America but throughout the world.

The idea of transformative change was clearly in the air, and in the 1970s many writers from a variety of backgrounds—including Jacob Needleman, Carl Rogers, Gregory Bateson, George Leonard, Willis Harman, Jonas Salk, José Argüelles, David Bohm, and Marilyn Ferguson—developed the theme from their own perspectives.[2] Networks of co-workers and kindred spirits came into being, each seeking to avoid the pitfalls of bureaucrati-

133

zation and depersonalization that characterize many of the institutions of modern society.

In certain professions, small groups met to discuss the implications of "transformational" ideas for their work. For example, in New York and California, psychologists formed an organization for Transpersonal Psychology. Similarly, a group of anthropologists and others seeking ways to develop the study of humankind further formed the Association for Transpersonal Anthropology and founded a journal appropriately named *Phoenix: Journal of Transpersonal Anthropology*. The Post-Graduate Center for Mental Health in New York City sponsored a small 1978 conference for professionals in psychology, education, literature, and science to meet with English physicist David Bohm and Indian sage J. Krishnamurti. And in California Buddhist teachers were invited to a gathering to help broaden the perspectives of American psychiatry.

Centers for holistic personal growth and spiritual exploration sprouted on the West Coast, in the Northeast, and in various other parts of the country. In the 1970s creative activity in the form of conferences, workshops, and retreats could be found at such places as Interface in Boston, the East-West Foundation in Brookline, Massachusetts, the Omega Institute in New Lebanon, New York, the Himalayan Institute in Chicago, the Lama Foundation in New Mexico, Lindisfarne (which has moved from its Long Island center to Colorado), the Naropa Institute in Boulder, Colorado, and the San Francisco Zen Center.

Mark Satin and the New World Alliance

The actual formation of a broad-based movement does not come easily. As an example of the process, let me trace the work of Mark Satin, who has devoted much time and energy since the late 1970s to develop an organizational structure for what can be called the "transformative change" movement.

Rather than be drafted to fight in the Vietnam War, which he strongly opposed, Satin fled to Canada for twelve years. After the conflict ended he returned to the United States, his outlook changed, determined to help build a better society. Instead of remaining embittered by having had to go into political exile,

Satin saw the need for a healing process, both within himself and within the United States.

Satin recalled that he had come to Canada "convinced that I hated the United States and everything in and about it, but . . . I (later) began to realize that I was engaged in a lover's quarrel with my country." He realized that living in Canada had given him the ability to see America as a whole and to work through his hatred: "It had given me exactly the perspective I needed to grow. I no longer wanted to bring socialism to our shores. Or any "ism" for that matter. Instead I wanted us to create a new and healing politics out of the indigenous social movements of our time."[3]

Satin saw that the ideas and energies of "various fringe movements—feminism, ecological, spiritual, human potential and the like"—had much to offer, but there was virtually no organized framework to give them political expression. He published his thoughts on the subject, first as a pamphlet and then in book form, in Canada. After receiving political amnesty, he traveled around the United States distributing his book, *New Age Politics,* and talking with a wide variety of people. As interest in his ideas grew, a major American publisher brought out a new edition of the book. Within a few years Satin had been instrumental in forming a coalition called the New World Alliance (NWA), whose stated objectives included the following:

The NWA seeks to break away from the old quarrels of "left against right" and help create a new consensus based on our heartfelt needs. It emphasizes personal growth—and nurturing others—rather than indiscriminate material growth. It advocates "human scale" institutions that function with human consideration and social responsibilities. It draws on the social movements of the recent past for new values like ecological responsibility, self-actualization and planetary cooperation and sharing. It draws on our conservative heritage for values such as personal responsibility, self-reliance, thrift, neighborliness and community. It draws from the liberal traditions a commitment to human and civil rights, economic equity and social justice. We call this synthesis "New World" politics.[4]

The thirty-nine members of the NWA Governing Council included teachers, futurists, environmentalists, feminists, think-tank members, and others from a variety of professional backgrounds.

A biweekly newsletter, *Renewal: New Values, New Politics,* edited by Satin was instituted as an ongoing forum and informational clearinghouse for the movement. Like the NWA itself, *Renewal* was based in Washington, D.C. Each of its founding sponsors—Ernest Callenbach, Willis Harman, Hazel Henderson, Karl Hess, Patricia Mische, Jeremy Rifkin, James Robertson (from Britain), Carl Rogers, and John Vasconcellos were accomplished writers, researchers, and activists in their fields. Vasconcellos also could put some of his ideas into practice as an innovative member of the California state legislature.

Renewal focused on the human growth, decentralist, and world order movements and sought "to critically assess and not just praise the books, pamphlets and articles that are relevant to those perspectives." As editor, Satin said he would try to avoid using words like *new age* and *transformational* and would try "to speak to every literate person, not just the already convinced."

The NWA sponsored a number of conferences and facilitated local and national networking. In 1981 the group put forward a "Transformational Platform," which was the first attempt to take ecological, decentralist, globalist, and human-growth ideas and translate them into a detailed, practical political platform with almost 300 specific proposals. Beginning in 1981 *Renewal* sponsored an annual Transformational Book Award (which has since been renamed the Political Book Award). The first such recognition, selected by a panel of seventy university teachers and research institute associates, went to Marilyn Ferguson for her book *The Aquarian Conspiracy.*[5]

Yet something was missing. Reflecting on the movement, Satin observed:

We have already created a coherent analysis, strategy, world-view, set of goals and economics that could serve as the basis for a political organization—and a badly underdeveloped practice.

We are engaged in theoretical-verbal overkill in exactly the same way the military people are engaged in stockpiling weapons and for the same kind of reasons. We are afraid to move. We don't know what to do, and we don't know what to do because we are afraid to try and fail. Men especially are afraid of failure. Some of us would rather lie or even die than to cop to failure.

But we can't work out an appropriate political strategy by sitting around and theorizing. There's only one way to create a viable political organization and that's to try and fail and learn and try and fail and learn until one day you do not fail.[6]

The above critique was presented at a panel discussion, "The Transformation: Is It Happening; What Is It Like?" which took place at a Conference of the Association for Humanistic Psychology in Washington, D.C., in August 1982. The estimated 400 people who crowded into the meeting room at American University did not hear the self-congratulatory "of course it's happening and it's wonderful" kind of presentations that many had become accustomed to. Instead, a startling reassessment took place, as each of the seven panelists put forth heartfelt criticisms of their own movement.[7]

One panelist, Walter Anderson, had coordinated the Political Ideology Network. He noted that the concept of transformation had been turning into a cliché. As soon as it entered the public dialogue, "it [became] as everything does in our society, a commodity." It also "has some of the quality of becoming what I think can rightfully be called a cult. The concept itself has become vague—it's not very clear to many people what we wish to transform and when, how much, where and how. I'm not at all sure we are bringing much clarity to the political dialogue."

Anderson went on to say that expecting a millennium of some sort has been very common throughout history. Religious movements have projected this kind of expectation and so have political movements.

As a matter of fact the kind of things that I hear people saying now about The Transformation are extremely similar to the kind of things people said about "The Revolution" when a large portion of American people were thinking in terms of some sort of American or world-wide version of Marxist revolution. There are the same sets of expectations of everything changing, with that change being inevitable, large, total, soon. Well, to come to my own position, I've found myself increasingly uncomfortable in the presence of transformational talk.

The fundamentalist Christians, Moral Majority, and right-wing conservatives are also "expecting an immediate and vast and inevitable change to take place in society, except that it is in many ways almost diametrically opposed to the one we expect. . . . As a matter of fact, some of those agendas include stamping us out, getting rid of these kinds of values that we think are inevitably going to sweep the world."

In sum, Anderson emphasized that he had grown tired of transformational talk. The word has taken on such overtones that "I prefer not to carry that particular load of baggage."

Another panel participant, Michael Marien, editor of the World Future Society's *Future Survey*, chided the transformation movement for the overuse of words like *network, caring, holistic, creativity, synergy,* and *feedback* and not coming to grips with the realities of competition, crime, and corporations. "Maybe they'll just go away," he quipped. He also emphasized that it is necessary to talk to more people than just the already converted. "If we are serious about a real transformation of values and perceptions, the world must know that desirable and practical alternatives exist."

The conference panelists' realistic appraisal of their movement's rhetorical overkill was in itself a healthy sign. Some rather painful recognitions had been expressed, often in the form of self-abnegating humor, but growth and a redefinition of purpose also took place. Satin announced that the September 6, 1982, issue would be the last for *Renewal,* and that subscribers would thereafter receive *The Tarrytown Letter,* another newsletter that deals with "new values and new politics."[8]

The NWA Governing Council dissolved and then reconstituted itself, all during that one weekend in August 1982. The alliance agreed to close its Washington, D.C., office but to keep the governing council together, and called for its next meeting to be held at Esalen in California. It was decided that the alliance thereafter would be an umbrella for a variety of entrepreneurial projects.

Satin himself has come to recognize that the New Age processes about which he had speculated do not have to be totally different from the past. "The point is not (just) to do things differently, as it is to comunicate with each other more honestly." He now sees the need to organize, to give structure to the generalized movement in existence: "With leadership, professionalism, will, an open heart, a searing honesty and plenty of friends to catch us when we fall, we can find our own path, forge ahead and create . . . the transformation." Satin said that he would again travel around the country to find ways "to communicate with the tens of millions of people out there who would move in our direction if they felt we were able to speak to their needs and fears."[9]

Soon Satin was busy laying the groundwork for another newsletter. It was conceived in the spirit of *Renewal,* but sought to be broader based, analyzing political and cultural developments beyond the confines of the transformationalist movement. Responding to the need for such a publication, hundreds of friends and supporters around the country pledged loans to put the newsletter on a sound financial footing.

The resulting newsletter, *New Options,* first appeared on February 27, 1984. Published every three weeks in Washington, D.C., it has a distinguished editorial board and welcomes contributions and feedback from its readers. *New Options* covers domestic and international events not readily discussed elsewhere and is written from a perspective that Satin describes as "post-conservative, post-liberal, post-socialist." It already has generated lively dialogue and is well on the way to becoming a useful forum for the discussion of new options.

The 1979 World Symposium on Humanity

The week-long World Symposium on Humanity, which was held in April 1979 simultaneously in Toronto, Los Angeles, and London, illustrated both the promise and the problems of the New Age movement in the 1970s.

The symposium's purpose was to discuss and to demonstrate the underlying unity of humanity. The event was hailed by its organizers as the foremost gathering of its kind. A diversity of excellent resource people took part. Those participating in the Toronto segment included scientist-educator Buckminster Fuller; poets Allen Ginsberg and Robert Bly; musicians Odetta, Paul Winter, Paul Horn, and David Avram; humanistic psychologists Jean Houston and June Singer; peace activist Paul Mayer; Native American spiritual leaders Thomas Banyacya and Mad Bear Anderson; architect Mimi Lobell; and teacher of macrobiotic living Michio Kushi. There was mime by Samuel Avital and melodic Hasidic chants by Rabbi Shlomo Carlbach. The lectures, workshops, and performances were virtually all of high quality.[10]

A festive atmosphere was created, with many booths presenting literature and other displays. Good food was available at reasonable cost, and Viktoras Kulvinskas, author of *Survival in the Twenty-First Century,* and friends distributed freshly grown sprouts. Small affinity-interest groups were created so that each of the thousand or so registrants could have familiar people to be in contact with each day.

But several problems emerged during the first days of the conference. One of the main attractions for a number of registrants was a Telstar satellite link among Los Angeles, Toronto, and London. At certain times of the day participants were to gather in the main auditorium and see, on a huge screen, speakers and events taking place in the other two cities. Promotional hype had focused on both the technological first to be achieved and its potential for spreading the transformational message of the New Age. But the linkup did not work, and other problems also arose, including the conference organizers' failure to meet some financial commitments. The plenary meetings, which were open to all, were in real disarray for several days. Recriminations were made, feelings were hurt, and the organizers were chastened. A number of people left early in disgust over the confusion. By midweek the whole conference was in danger of disintegrating, but fortunately cooler heads, led by twenty or so Native Americans, helped save the day. They spoke imploringly of how incongruous it was that during a conference heralding the unity of humankind such disharmony was taking place. Their pleas had a sobering effect on the audience. A process of healing and reconciliation was soon in evidence at the open meetings. On the last day a live contact was made with the Los Angeles conference, but not on the huge videoscreen. Symbolically, the exchange of heartfelt greetings came through the humbler means of shortwave radio. It was probably for the best that the Telstar hookup did not work. There had been more than enough to do without sitting bleary-eyed for several hours daily in front of a huge television screen.

The closing moments of the conference were very moving for all. The Native Americans who had been so instrumental in pulling the fragmented conference together again helped the other participants to reflect on the gathering's broader implications and the work to be done after people returned home. Then everyone formed a huge circle and linked arms in a final sharing. Although a number of problems had surfaced at the conference, some valuable lessons were learned in dealing with them openly.

The 1984 Human Unity Conference

The spirit of strength and joy among people meeting to share deep convictions without being fanatical, that Erich Fromm envisioned in 1968, was present in large measure at the eleventh annual Human Unity Conference (HUC) held in Boston from July 19 to 22, 1984. Over 600 participants came together on the campus of Simmons College to explore the theme "The Healing of the Nations: A Personal Purpose."[11]

The human unity concept was initiated in 1974 by the respected Indian teacher Sant Kirpal Singh, who convened a World Conference on the Unity of Man in New Delhi to build greater understanding between representatives of all the world's religious and spiritual traditions. Since then conferences have been held in a different country each year, including Mexico, Austria, Spain, Canada, Brazil, England, and the United States. Each conference has had a different theme; yet all have been related to the human unity concept. The Boston conclave was coordinated by Elaine Gagné, Ed.D., and Laurence Krantz, M.D., directors of the Whole Health Institute centered in Epping, New Hampshire.

The conference was billed as a celebration of awakening to global unity and understanding—a gathering of people to express the "creative integrity which will help heal the rifts" dividing humankind. Each person was invited to leave his or her occupational label at the door.

Primarily North Americans attended, but there were at least several people present from every continent. The HUC is nonprofit, and all the participants—even the organizers—paid their own way. An impressive variety of people took part—including a good number who are doing innovative work in the healing arts, counseling, teaching, and community service. As at other such conferences, however, there were few if any representatives of the impoverished half of the world's population.

In the conference plenary sessions and workshops many expressed the need "to take personal responsibility to let peace and harmony become a reality on this planet." Music, dance, and drama on the theme of unity within diversity helped provide an atmosphere of celebration. Among the artists who took part were New England musicians such as Do'a—World Music Ensemble and On Wings of Song. An important feature of the conference was small discussion groups of up to twelve people who met twice daily. These Circles of Friends provided an atmosphere of trust and support in which in-depth discussions took place and conference participants got to know one another better.

The purpose of the conference was also exemplified by a presentation featuring William Ury and Marc Sarkady of the Harvard Law School's Nuclear Negotiations Project. Both are working on ways to manage crises and mediate disputes between the superpowers. One means is the creative use of new technologies. An innovative approach in this area is the slow-scan video, which will allow considerably more ongoing audiovisual contact between groups such as the Nuclear Negotiations Project and its Soviet counterpart at the Moscow-based Institute for the Study of the United States and Canada. The Harvard group is coordinating its efforts with the "Spacebridge project" sponsored by the Association for Humanistic Psychology.

John Graham, an ex–Foreign Service officer who used to plan nuclear strategy for NATO, was another of the conference speakers. He now seeks common ground with the leaders and people of the USSR and spends his time looking for fellow human giraffes— people willing "to stick their necks out"—taking the lead in finding ways to prevent nuclear war.

Bridging the Gap between Activism and Introspection

A number of people involved in the political or social change movements of the 1960s did not condone the introspective mode of the post-Vietnam era. Some interpreted noninvolvement in movement politics as a cop-out, and felt values such as voluntary simplicity were simply irrelevant. Some saw their friends convert to what appeared to be bizarre religious practices and therefore viewed New Age talk as an opiate that deactivated and misguided people. Unreceptive to the positive side, they focused on aspects that reinforced their negative views. Similarly, some of the new alternatives people grew increasingly impatient with those who expressed political concerns.

Ways are needed to bridge the gap between those "sixties-style activists" and "seventies and eighties New Agers." Both have qualities that can be of value in the exploration of new paths for positive change within society. A willingness to be tolerant can lead to deeper mutual respect and understanding. Fresh modes of expression should be developed out of the best qualities of both activism and introspection. New Agers who in the 1980s are calling for broad-based coalitions to help structure their ideas exemplify those moving toward a broader common ground. And more activists are coming to recognize that politics in the broader sense involves all aspects of a person's life.

Becoming more attuned to what the founder of the Society of Friends, George Fox, once called "that still small voice within" does not require withdrawal from active social participation. Bryn Beorse—a Norwegian student of Sufism and a scientist-engineer who has pioneered a technology to extract solar energy from the ocean's waters—reminds us that we don't have to give up working for peace in the world while working on our own growth. "You don't get any peace within yourself without working in the world and with the world."[12]

Modest beginnings of transformative changes are underway in America, but much more remains to be done. The term *transformation* itself has been used by some to describe what has been happening in their own lives. Growth and in some instances remarkable changes have occurred. It would appear, though, that few individuals have completed the metamorphosis into New Age butterflies. The "peak experiences" of which Abraham Maslow wrote are in reality more a peek into what can be, but has not yet been fully actualized. The development of humility, a quality more easily spoken about than manifested, is important in this regard. Those who are undergoing lasting changes will not have to speak about how "high" their consciousness has been raised—their actions and demeanor will speak for themselves. Poet Robert Bly provides a good rule of thumb: "If a person is talking about consciousness check out his daily life. See how he lives."[13]

Notes

1. Erich Fromm, *Revolution of Hope* (New York: Harper and Row, 1968).

2. For a discussion of these authors and their work see the chapter "Premonitions of Transformation" in Marilyn Ferguson, *Aquarian Conspiracy: Personal and Social Transformation in the 1980s* (Los Angeles: J. B. Tarcher, 1980), 45–63.

3. Quoted from the introductory "A Personal Word" (pp. 1–3) to Mark Satin, *New Age Politics: Healing Self and Society* (New York: Delta, 1979).

4. Excerpted from a NWA communiqué of November 1980.

5. Certificates of "respect and appreciation" were also given to four runner-up books: Alvin Toffler, *The Third Wave;* Kirkpatrick Sale, *Human Scale;* Erich Jantsch, *The Self-Organizing Universe;* and Jeremy Rifkin, *Entropy.* The 1982 award went to Duane Elgin's *Voluntary Simplicity;* and in 1983 the recognition was given to Paul Hawkens, James Oglivy, and Peter Schwartz for *Seven Tomorrows.*

6. *Renewal: New Values, New Politics,* no. 28 (September 6, 1982).

7. Edited versions of these talks appeared in the September 6, 1982, issue of *Renewal.* The excerpts in the following paragraphs are taken from this source.

8. *The Tarrytown Letter* is a publication of the Tarrytown Group, which was cofounded by anthropologist Margaret Mead and businessman Robert Schwartz. It has 12,000 subscribers worldwide.

9. *Renewal* (September 6, 1982): 1.

10. The *Prospects for Humanity* series, moderated by Dr. Patricia Hunt-Perry, had five 1-hour segments: Energy and Technology, Community and Culture, Evolution and Education, Consciousness and Health, and Justice and Religion. It was prepared with a grant from the National Endowment for the Humanities in April–June, 1979. The films, along with full transcripts, are available through WOSU-TV 34, Columbus, Ohio.

11. Information in this section is drawn from materials put out by the conference organizers and from personal observations.

12. Bryn Beorse, "In Search of Mystic Balance," *New Age Journal* (March 1978): 76.

13. From a talk given by Robert Bly at the University of Rhode Island Honors Colloquium on "The Human Spirit" on October 20, 1977.

Chapter 8

The Potential within the Seed

We often tend to get caught up in the present moment and to exaggerate the potential long-range significance of current trends. During the heady atmosphere of the late 1960s and early 1970s, some observers envisaged a "greening of America" almost around the corner, sparked by a dawning new wave of consciousness that would rapidly permeate and change the overall direction of our culture. Then, with the publicized demise of the flower children and the aftermath of Vietnam and Watergate a counterwave of pessimism and cynicism crept in, a reaction against the somewhat effulgent earlier optimism. Presumably, enough time has elapsed so that we can begin to look at those years with a more balanced perspective.

In this endeavor we have explored the values, work, and commitments of a number of people and groups who sought positive approaches to life in the nuclear era. One can ask: Have their ideas and activities had much effect on the broader society? There is no simple answer.

Despite setbacks, however, there have been some encouraging incremental signs of more democratization within the political system in recent years: The increasingly significant role of women in both major parties was highlighted when Walter Mondale selected Geraldine Ferraro as his vice-presidential running mate in

1984. Black Americans have made inroads in municipal politics and have been elected mayors of a number of major American cities. The formation of the Rainbow Coalition and the presidential candidacy of the Reverend Jesse Jackson, accompanied by a widespread voter registration drive among poor black Americans and other minorities, also augurs well.

Yet there are many sobering realities to be faced. The inflation rate has been reduced considerably, but unemployment among the poor and minorities remains high. There is more homelessness in America than at any time since the Great Depression, and many farmers are losing their land. The gap between the wealthiest and the poorest fifths of the population continues to grow; and the nation is confronted with runaway budgetary deficits. Governmental policies toward our neighbors in Central America remain muddled, to say the least. Relations with the Soviet Union have deteriorated, and the nuclear arms race continues to escalate.

But instead of focusing on our inability for the most part to affect the immediate direction of national policy, we can take another perspective. Social critics have aptly noted that the 1970s was a time for widespread excesses of individualism. It was therefore all the more important for those who rejected egoistic values to follow their own drumbeat and pursue life-giving alternatives. Those who did not define self-interest narrowly helped keep the spark of idealism alive while they continued the time-honored tradition of inquiring into what constitutes a qualitatively good life. Many of the values they espoused transcend conservative or liberal labels.

One can read of various endeavors toward self-understanding and societal reorientation and still respond, "So what, things are going on just as before." Yet without those who stand up against social injustices, and without pathfinders to explore constructive modes of change, things assuredly would be worse. Fortunately, the search for societal and cultural sanity was pursued by many who belied the "me-decade" stereotype. And regardless of the vicissitudes of national politics or existing economic structures, this quest continues.

The experiments with various alternatives in the 1970s, like those of previous decades, are laboratories which over time can be of considerable benefit to the broader society. In the political sphere, for example, almost all the progressive reforms in the past century began with small third parties or independent movements. The Democratic Socialists of America and the Citizens Party are very much in that tradition. Whether or not they eventually attract larger followings, or even continue to exist, has little to do with their present value of keeping alive and enhancing the concepts of participatory democracy and social justice.

Starting in the early 1970s small groups of citizens began to call attention to the dangers of nuclear power and the general threat to the environment and human health of excessive chemical pollution. The nation is indebted to those who first raised awareness in these areas, and who helped mobilize public response when crises like Three Mile Island and Love Canal occurred. Rather than succumb to psychic numbness, some also chose to challenge the rationale for the nuclear arms race. In doing so they acted in the tradition of nonviolent dissent and exercised the basic rights so important to the vital functioning of a democracy.

Organizations like HOME, New Communities Inc., and the National Sharecroppers Fund provide new sources of hope for the rural poor. While serving as models for improving conditions in the backwaters of America, they also pertain to the movements for human dignity and economic upliftment in the less developed areas of the world. There can be beneficial exchanges, for example, between American groups and the *sarvodaya* village self-upliftment programs of India and Ceylon.

The citizens' movements in many villages, towns, and cities that Harry Boyte termed a "backyard revolution" were a major source for positive change in the 1970s. Some of these groups have developed further and successfully dealt with the inevitable problems that arise from growth. Others temporarily served their purposes, but have not been sustained themselves. Community projects in the cities, such as the sweat equity programs pioneered in several New York City boroughs, are encouraging illustrations of what can be done in even the most impoverished urban settings.

The Movement for a New Society in cooperation with the Philadelphia Life Center provides a successful example of how urban-based groups can develop cooperative living situations. Its participants are also engaged in a variety of social and political causes, which extend from community-based concerns to national and transnational issues.

Intentional communities such as Twin Oaks, Cerro Gordo, The Farm, and Ananda, all have had their growing pains, of course; economic problems and interpersonal conflicts have to be dealt with in small communities as well as in the outside world. But each offers unique innovative experiences for their members and are willing to share what they have learned with the broader society.

Literally thousands of cooperative ventures sprang up in the 1960s and 1970s. Most have had a life span averaging perhaps a few years. Some were reconstituted in other forms, while others discontinued operation. Whether or not a particular organizational structure maintains itself is not as important as whether during its life it served a beneficial purpose for those who participated. Longevity of an institution is not necessarily the most important criterion for measuring its societal contributions, although it is certainly the easiest factor to quantify.

Today's food and health consciousness trend was started primarily by "new alternatives" people in the food cooperative movement. This awareness is moving into the public at large and is reflected in the growing financial success of health food stores and the natural foods sections of supermarkets. For those interested in spreading the work-sharing, communitarian, and egalitarian decision-making aspects of cooperatives it is disappointing that the co-op movement has not grown much in the past several years. Yet the general public continues to benefit from the ongoing experiences of cooperatives. For instance, practices such as honest informational labeling of product ingredients, pioneered decades ago by co-ops, gained the status of law in the 1970s.

A growing number of people have realized that one can be of service to others and meet one's own basic needs at the same time. A few examples are representative: The Community for Creative Non-Violence and the Catholic Worker help to care for the poor and homeless of the cities. ACORN (Association of Community Organization for Reform Now), CLOC (Community Labor Organizing Coalition), Common Cause, and the Public Interest Research Groups (PIRGs) assist communities to organize for social reform and consumer justice. Human bonds are developed by those serving abroad in the Peace Corps, World Friends Service Committee, and Oxfam, and by medical-care personnel of a dozen religious denominations. Church and community groups assisted in the 1970s to resettle refugees from the Vietnam War in the United States. In the 1980s thousands of people from various religious communities are breaking the law but following their consciences to provide sanctuary for "illegal" political refugees from El Salvador and Guatemala.

Many others give of their time, resources, and love working with the less fortunate in their own communities. This service, whether recognized or given anonymously, helps enrich the fabric of life in America.

Some Sources of Hope

Cultural developments, unlike calendars, cannot be neatly divided into decades. With the passage of time we will gain a broader perspective on the events of the 1970s. It might be appropriate to turn now to some thoughts about moving toward a viable future.

In a time when one can be overwhelmed by the many negative events that occur daily in the world, it is encouraging to hear the views of those who see the positive aspects of human possibility. Affirmative vision sometimes gets reduced to simplistic clichés, however, and there are no ready-made blueprints for a "New Age." As poet-futurist David Spangler aptly put it: "When it comes to the evolution of a new culture there are no experts—but we can figure it out together and build as we go along. The New Age is something that must be lived into beingness. It is not a product to be manufactured like a new car."[1]

Today we speak of an energy crisis, as we continue rapidly to deplete the planet's nonrenewable resources. Not only are many physical resources being squandered, but much human potential is as well. A lot of cultural energy is lost in defining ourselves as separate, unconnected beings. The real energy crisis begins within the human psyche. An abundance of human energy can be generated by working together in common cause.

As we mutually enhance and empower one another, synergy can come into play. This principle was employed by Buckminster Fuller in the construction of his geodesic domes. In essence it holds that the sum is greater than the total of its component parts. The concept is also applicable to efforts involving human interaction. If each member of a group puts forth his or her best efforts, the result will be greater than the mere sum of individual inputs. Also, the synergy—shared energy—that the collective effort has produced will return more than the original investment of time, efforts, or resources to the participating individuals. To use a rather crude banking metaphor, each can receive not only the standard rate of interest, but a bonus dividend as well. Understanding and applying this principle would help release constant source of human energy and creativity.

Energy can be expressed in many ways, including the sheer physical strength, agility, and sometimes joy of athletic performance. Unfortunately, the Los Angeles Olympics, as the Moscow games of 1980, did not include the athletes of all the world's nations because of reciprocal boycotts. The 1984 Olympics were also marred by excesses of commercialism and flag-waving nationalism. Yet there were powerful moments that stirred the human spirit.

The Olympic torch had crossed the breadth of the country, proudly carried by thousands of runners and witnessed by millions more. It was deeply moving when the granddaughter of the great 1936 olympian Jesse Owens entered the colosseum carrying the torch, ran a complete lap holding it aloft, and then passed it on to former decathalon champion Rafer Johnson, who completed the lighting ceremony. It also touched the heart when the olympians from many lands linked hands to sing together: "Reach out and touch somebody's hand, make this world a better place if you can."

Healing energy also plays a vital role. The United States emerged from the Vietnam War a divided and wounded nation. Confused veterans returned to an indifferent reception from the public and government alike. Many veterans still suffer the after-effects of their traumatic experiences in the war. The unveiling in Washington of the Memorial Wall marked a significant milestone for the veterans, their families and friends, and the nation as a whole. In its quiet dignity, the black granite wall bears witness to many personal stories, and to a process of healing that is now underway.

Energy also takes the form of active social and political protest when the machinery of government remains unresponsive to the more modulated voices of reason. This became the only recourse during the long, frustrating years of Vietnam, and it may well be needed again as the situation in Central America becomes increasingly critical.

The development of a new "species consciousness" by humankind involves the participation of people throughout the world; it cannot be done in the Western nations alone. Indeed, a positive view of human potential is a necessity if widespread change is to be achieved. Such a perspective energizes a man like Robert Muller, who serves as U.N. Undersecretary General coordinating thirty-two U.N. agencies and programs. He is known among his colleagues as the United Nations' "philosopher of hope." In his latest book, *New Genesis: Shaping a Global Spirituality,* Muller foresees the dawning of a global age and the development of a sense of brotherhood and sisterhood of all people.[2] Despite all the present international conflicts and problems, Muller sees the nations slowly overcoming their narrowness. As incipient signs of an emerging worldwide consciousness, he points to global conferences on disarmament, ecology, the aged, the malnourished, and "the year of the child," all of which took place for the first time in the past decade. Muller has had an active role in preparing the groundwork for such conferences. Also, much success has been achieved in projects undertaken by U.N. agencies such as the World Health Organization. In *New Genesis* Muller puts forth a number of proposals to strengthen the United Nations. He wishes to see it become effective in helping humanity realize its birthright to live in peace. The infectious faith and optimism of a person like Robert Muller calls to mind a line from a Denise

Levertov poem, that hope is "like a clump of irises which will cease to flower unless you distribute the clusters of roots."

Others with an international orientation also feel that affirmative thought is a prelude to positive action. For example, in 1981 the first meeting of what has since been called the Planetary Initiative for the World We Choose took place. Little noted at the time, the conclave was sponsored by an ad hoc coalition of five groups—Planetary Citizens, the Association for Humanistic Psychology, Global Education Associates, the Club of Rome, and the U.N. Association for New South Wales (Australia). One commentator noted: "It wasn't exactly an auspicious time for an endeavor based on optimism. *The Bulletin of Atomic Scientists* had, at the end of 1980, just moved their Doomsday Clock from seven minutes to four minutes before midnight, citing 'tragic destabilization' and a world 'moving unevenly but inexorably closer to nuclear disaster.' " But "at a time when optimists might well have been reaching for their cyanide tablets" the Planetary Initiative group assembled in Stony Point, New York.[3]

The secretariat for the venture was the Planetary Citizens, an international group started in the early 1970s by Donald Keys, Norman Cousins, and the late U.N. Secretary General U Thant of Burma. The Planetary Initiative seeks to organize an international constituency that will focus attention on such pressing problems as the arms race, hunger, overpopulation, pollution, and political exploitation. But rather than just protesting against these injustices, the initiative's organizing manual calls for developing a more positive identity: "Most people tend to know what they are against but not what they are for. A vision of the world we want is needed if we are eventually to arrive there."

Several hundred organizations have already linked up with the initiative, and a Planetary Congress was held on the summer solstice (June 21) of 1983. One of the movement's basic goals is to "bring the planetary issues home." Rather than just creating another centralized network, the initiative wants to act as a catalyst for activities on the local and regional levels as well.

Organizations such as the Planetary Initiative and the Washington, D.C.–based Search for Common Ground are working to identify areas of commonality between individuals and groups from a variety of backgrounds and political inclinations. Out of the discovery of mutual interests can come the basis for working together.

There can be many approaches to creating a more peaceful world. For example, innovative work in the United States is being done in the vital area of peace conversion by economist Seymour Melman and activist-writer Joanne Macy. Sociologist Elise Boulding is a leading advocate for a National Peace Academy. Proponents of a World Peace Tax Fund have tirelessly waged an uphill struggle to gain congressional support. Among the members of Congress itself, Representative Ron Dellums of Berkeley, California, for many years has actively supported these causes.

It has been said that artists, poets, writers, and thinkers are "the antennae of the race—the sensitive ones in the human family who sense like radar what is coming, yet is unseen to most of us." With us are living voices from the past—William Blake and his vision of the New Jerusalem and Walt Whitman's *Leaves of Grass*, which sings of America's potential. Today there are writer Maya Angelou, the musical groups Do'a—A New World Ensemble—and Sumitra [Good Friends], Sweet Honey in the Rock, and many others to help awaken us to our common humanity.

One does not have to place a premium on things that are seemingly new. A continuing challenge is to discover what is of enduring value from our past heritage and to determine what might be adapted to present needs. Having this in mind, we can learn much from the life experiences of others. I have pointed to people whose lives have been instructive—Elisabeth Kübler-Ross, Helen and Scott Nearing, Wendell Berry, E. F. Schumacher, Juanita and Wally Nelson, Dorothy Day, Myles Horton, and others who have done much of their creative work as they advanced in years. Remaining young in spirit as they mature in wisdom, they are often an inspiration for those of a later generation seeking credible role models.

America today is at a crossroads. Without discretion, the "American dream" can easily become an ersatz one, leading on the personal level to a desire for excessive wealth and power, and on the societal level to a nation with little purpose or direction. At its best, the American dream to me could more accurately be described as a vision. Unlike a dream, which has an ephemeral quality, a vision connotes a deeper level of truth. This vision is of a society that allows each person—regardless of race, religion, or class—the opportunity to fulfill his or her unique aspirations. It is of a land where people care for and help one another, where children can grow up safely and realize their full potential as human beings. This American vision is one in which each person has the inalienable right to live without fear or want. To paraphrase Gandhi, this world has enough to meet each one's need, but not enough to meet anyone's greed. The same applies to the United States.

Historically, America represents the promise of freedom and opportunity. It was a beacon that attracted millions to its shores. Many in the world still look to America for moral leadership, and are disappointed when it is lacking. "Let freedom ring," as Dr. Martin Luther King once eloquently implored, can yet be a rallying call for America, and for all peoples in the world yearning to be free.

With its present material abundance and military might, America is susceptible to the pitfalls that result from an arrogance of power. Concurrently, it is challenged to develop more fully the humility and compassion that are evidences of true greatness and strength.

All around this planet voices are calling out to be heard—mothers in Northern Ireland who see their children embittered by years of civil strife, people in the African Sahel crying for food, citizens calling for the right of self-determination in Eastern Europe and Afghanistan and in Nicaragua and El Salvador, people of color in South Africa seeking human dignity, political "prisoners of conscience" in a hundred countries, and those throughout the world burdened economically and psychologically by the ever-increasing armaments race. What happens within the United States in the next few years will greatly influence this nation's capacity for leadership in helping to resolve these critical issues of planetary concern.

A broad spectrum of people in various ways are harbingers, laying the groundwork for reorientation within American society. They include:

Those doing pioneering work on the "urban frontier," reconstituting neighborhoods and helping the powerless to help themselves

Those who are striving to alleviate poverty and promote human dignity in rural America

Those engaged in the ongoing struggle for basic human rights and social justice

Those developing various forms of cooperatives and exploring innovative approaches to living and working together in community

Those who are simplifying their living and consumption patterns, to improve the quality of both their own lives and those of others

Those in the healing arts who are taking an holistic approach in their vocations

Those developing and utilizing alternative, renewable, and nonpolluting energy resources

Those engaged in innovative and serviceful ways of earning a livelihood and helping others to do the same

Those protecting the public interest against abuses by powerful groups or faceless bureaucracies

Scholars and journalists probing to the roots of the issues they investigate

Artists, writers, poets, and others opening new perspectives to enhance our appreciation of life

Educators encouraging in their students the spark of honest inquiry

Religious leaders who teach by example and not by precept

Scientists and other explorers of outer and inner space increasing our understanding of the physical and metaphysical dimensions of the universe

Those practicing the art of politics with integrity and compassion

Those striving to conserve the natural environment and encourage respect for all life-forms

Those working for nonviolent approaches to conflict resolution and a more peaceful world

But however significant these individuals and groups may be as explorers of constructive alternatives or as catalysts for social change, they collectively remain a rather small minority of the total population. In short, they cannot themselves revitalize America. For any significant national reorientation to take place they must be joined by substantial numbers of those from what might be termed mainstream or middle America, people who work in the nation's mines and mills, farms, offices, and businesses. Those advocating change should be receptive to the concerns and fears of everyday working people. Nonthreatening ways must be found to let people see for themselves that there are viable alternatives.

There is considerable interest in finding ways to regenerate American society at a time when established institutions and power structures have lost some of their credibility and capacity for leadership. But the overall approach has to be inclusive and not exclusive, and a place should be found for everyone who wishes to participate.

In 1776 Thomas Paine wrote that "we have the power to begin the world again." He and those of like mind, seen by many of their day as extremists, helped bring about the American Revolution. But what we are talking about today, more than 200 years later, is something more complex than gaining political independence. It is a struggle that cannot be won with bullets and barricades. It involves a different kind of revolution—the working through of a process, and not just a final climactic political act. Re-volution in the full sense, literally a complete turning around, appears necessary if we are not only to survive as a people but to become a more humane society. Such a revolution cannot be achieved in a classical, Marxian way. A class-based revolution, even if it could "succeed," would not get to the core of America's present problems. What is most needed is an opening of the heart, a deepening of insights, and a willingness to listen empathetically to others. Such a "turning" by a substantial portion of the population would be truly revolutionary.

In this light Sant Darshan Singh writes that the greatest revolutionary change can only be wrought by a change of attitude within the human heart: "We are witnessing the dawn of a spiritual revolution. By definition, such a revolution, unlike political, social or economic ones, cannot be enforced from without. It is an inner revolution which centers on a change of consciousness. We cannot convert others, we can only convert ourselves."[4]

As the traditional boundaries of time and space recede, it becomes necessary to give more attention to the art of communication on a person-to-person level. This involves being able to acknowledge the humanity of each person with whom one comes into contact. Dr. Jean Houston, whose professional work has centered on human communication, believes in the importance of developing empathic listening. To be reached and acknowledged by another, especially during times of confusion, disorientation, or grief, is clearly analogous to being given a dose of warm sunshine. "The process of healing and growth is quickened when another's warmth is freely given." Human interchanges in their fullest sense "involve an exchange of essences, an awakening, an exchange of vitality back and forth. The partners in true meetings discover themselves broadened, deepened, nourished."[5]

Also essential in the quest for communication are the qualities of love and truthfulness. In this context David Spangler describes love as "that willingness, that courage, and that openness to create a space within which my bounds and your bounds have a chance to dissolve, a space in which we become willing to be vulnerable with each other."[6]

In his illuminating *The Road Less Traveled: A New Psychology of Love, Traditional Values and Spiritual Growth*, psychotherapist M. Scott Peck defines love as: "The will to extend one's self for the purpose of nurturing one's own or another's spiritual growth." Love is that "holy spirit" which can heal the divisiveness within the trinity of body, mind and spirit.[7]

In the words of the courageous Bishop Desmond Tutu who received the 1984 Nobel Peace Prize for his opposition to apartheid in South Africa: "We know that goodness can overcome evil, that light overcomes darkness and love can overcome hatred."

Basically, we are envisaging a society in which each person, in the words of Dr. Martin Luther King, can develop a "new sense of somebodyness" and in which people of all backgrounds can live, work, and share together for the common good.

Ours is a time that needs a universal process of healing—within individuals, between people, among races and nations. In saying this, it would be remiss not to look briefly at a currently sensitive area that affects the quality of human relationships and has deep implications for individual self-understanding.

Every human being possesses complementary life-energies, which have been described in various cultural settings as yin/yang, intuitive/rational, feminine/masculine, and so on. Jungian psychologist June Singer has noted that American men and women today are expressing previously underdeveloped sides of their natures and taking roles historically assigned to the opposite sex. Women are becoming more active in the business world outside the home, and men are beginning to take a larger share of child rearing responsibilities. A male does not have to give up his masculinity, but can just allow himself the welcome relief of being able to express his own innate warmth and gentleness.[8]

In societal terms there is much to be done to emancipate ourselves from what Elizabeth Dodson Gray in her recent book has called "the patriarchal trap."[9] She assures us that she does not wish to see matriarchy replace patriarchy, for that "would not be any improvement." Yet "our problem now is that survival as a species on the earth is threatened by the spread of a monoculture—a scientific and industrial and militaristic culture created out of the male consciousness." The "male" aspect has been dominant over at least the past 3,000 years, while the authentic feminine side of our consciousness is just beginning to emerge. As Elizabeth Janeway has observed, women themselves are "between myth and morning," just awakening into a truly "female" consciousness. Because of this situation, Gray concludes that: "If we desire genuinely to balance the human perception of reality, we must all—males and females—nurture the birth of authentic women's consciousness." When the "balance is set straight," all will benefit from the result.

An inclusive society fosters the recognition that every person should be respected, and that each has a contribution to make. There is a role for everyone, including, of course, corporate business executives. To say this may sound a little incongruous, or even patronizing, after having cited a number of instances in which people seeking social justice have had to confront the abuses and insensitivities of "corporate America." Yet there have been enlightened capitalists, starting with Robert Owen in Wales 175 years ago. Current enterprises like those of F. Scott Bader Inc. in Great Britain and the Vermont Castings Company, recognize that it makes good business sense to be concerned for the well-being of one's employees, to take pride in the quality of one's products, and to be socially responsible.

Those who control the corporate boardrooms and own the stocks and bonds are realizing that as private citizens they want to breathe fresh air, drink clear water, and eat food grown in nonpolluted soil. But by their very nature, large bureaucratic and profit-oriented structures tend to be impersonal. This necessitates the careful public monitoring of questionable conduct that could adversely affect society. Encouragement and positive recognition should be given whenever corporations and financial institutions engage in socially responsible activities such as funding scholarship programs in inner-city schools and supporting cultural enrichment programs.

Here are a few examples of how the qualities and characteristics I have ascribed to many of those seeking positive alternatives in the 1970s and 1980s could help bring about significant changes in the broader society: (1) Develop a life pattern based more on voluntary simplicity so that America uses its resources more wisely and is less of a drain on the rest of the world. We would then be more sympathetic toward others, create fewer antagonisms, and lessen the divisions between haves and have-nots at home and abroad. (2) Learn to work together in smaller, human-scaled groups to hone the skills of participatory democracy. Support alternative institutions that emphasize cooperation, mutual aid, and inclusiveness to help lay the groundwork for a more egalitarian, nonsexist, and nonracist society. (3) Recognize the importance of life-affirming behavior to help lessen environmental pollution and despoilment. (4) Become centered, more fully integrated human beings with a greater sense of self-worth. This will resolve many of the personal problems that stem from the alienation and frustration rampant in society today. (5) Take more responsibility for our individual health care and general well-being. This will also help cut back on rapidly rising medical costs, which threaten the Medicare and Social Security systems. (6) Use nonviolent means of conflict resolution to settle differences in a world currently divided along class, racial, religious, and national lines and facing the ultimate danger of nuclear holocaust.

"For Everything There Is a Season"

When Neil Armstrong took the first tentative steps of his moon walk in 1969, the public imagination was captivated by the new technologies that the venture into outer space had made possible. But for some the extraterrestrial adventure also dramatically underscored the need for equivalent attention to the exploration of "inner space." The ongoing quest for self-knowledge has taken on a new urgency in an era marked by the uncontrolled proliferation of weapons of mass destruction. Humankind needs to know more about its own complex nature if the products of scientific development are to be wisely used.

The remarkably beautiful photos of the whole earth and its life-giving atmosphere from beyond our planet gave us a fresh perspective. They visually demonstrated that humanity and other terrestrial life-forms are common travelers aboard spaceship Earth, and that the lives and destinies of all are inextricably linked. Basic questions about the meaning of life and the purpose of human existence were raised anew. Although many were drawn by the end of the 1970s to an obsession with Space Invaders and other videogames, others were challenged to ponder anew the eternal introspective queries posed in the title of Gauguin's painting: "What Have We Come From? What Are We? Where Are We Going?"

A recognition is thus emerging in today's fragmented world of the need to reintegrate the branches of the mythic tree of knowledge, to find the common trunk and subsurface roots from which science, art, religion, and philosophy spring. This reintegration is necessary, not only to ensure our very physical survival, but for our mental, spiritual, and cultural revitalization as well. What is called for is a weaving together of the often disparate strands of knowledge from various fields into a fabric that will better enable us to understand ourselves and the life-support systems in which we live.

As we approach the year 2000 A.D. with all its millennial overtones, questions are often raised about the future of humankind. In what basic direction is our world heading? And what might our lives be like in the years to come? Among the responses to these fundamental questions two increasingly polarized points of view have emerged. In broad terms, one viewpoint holds that great disasters and chaos lie ahead; the other contends that transformative responses are emerging to meet the challenges of our era and that somehow humankind can learn to resolve its differences and live peacefully.

The proponents of both scenarios can muster "evidence" for their cases. One position can present a compelling argument based on the inhumanities and suffering throughout the world, including the denial of basic rights and dignity to many men, women, and children. Its case is further substantiated by statistical projections of current trends, which point to more wars, overpopulation, famine, environmental pollution, and the increasing possibility of the ultimate humanmade catastrophe, a devastating nuclear war.

Yet those with a more optimistic vision adhere to the belief that the forces of life will yet prevail, that over the next several decades humanity will become increasingly aware of and will act on the necessity to lay the groundwork for a peaceful planetary order. This alternative perspective is less visible to the general public and receives less media attention. It draws on the innate human capacity to care for and cooperate with one another and is evidenced by the consideration that many people extend daily. One thing both viewpoints agree on is that people and governments cannot continue a "business as usual" attitude and expect to pass through the mounting challenges of our era unscathed.

Looming above all other matters is the continuing threat of nuclear holocaust. There has been an increase in public awareness of the issue in recent years. But individuals, once alerted to the danger, may feel overwhelmed and wonder if they can do anything to affect the outcome of such an immense problem. Perhaps the following story can offer some encouragement.

In his book *Lifetide: The Biology of the Unconscious*, biologist Lyall Watson reported an interesting chain of events that took place after sweet potatoes were first introduced to a tribe of monkeys on a small island off the coast of Japan.[10] The monkeys were interested in the potatoes, but didn't like the dirt and grit on the skins. Then one day an ingenious young monkey found a creative solution to the problem—she carried a potato down to the stream and washed off the dirt and sand. The monkey then enjoyed eating clean potatoes and soon showed what she had done to her mother and some playmates. The parent appeared skeptical, but the younger monkeys quickly picked up the innovation. The practice gradually spread to some of the adults. Then, after a substantial number of the tribe had begun washing the potatoes before eating them, a turning point was reached— within a short time all the monkeys were doing it. The rate at which the new practice spread grew from an arithmetic toward a geometric progression. When that anonymous "hundredth monkey" had developed the potato-washing awareness, the practice had seemingly become part of the collective consciousness of the entire tribe. Not surprisingly, Watson was enthusiastic in his description of what had taken place.

In reading Ken Keyes's delightful little book *The Hundredth Monkey* an obvious question comes to mind: If monkeys can learn and teach one another a new and appropriate way to get rid of unwanted grit on sweet potatoes, doesn't humankind have the capacity to find successful ways to dispose of our relatively newly acquired but highly distasteful nuclear weaponry?[11]

While studying the evolution of life-forms on this planet, scientists have come on instances when, as an old order or process is breaking down, a sudden shift occurs, a leap into a higher form or order. Obviously, rapid change must occur if humanity is to avert the nuclear catastrophe toward which we could be heading. Only in this instance it is not a biological adaptation that is necessary, but a collective shift of awareness accompanied by appropriate social and political action. The emergency situation with which we are confronted is far more critical than whether or not to eat gritty potatoes—our response to this new challenge may involve the very survival of our species.

Where might this emerging awareness stem from? On one level it can develop from an "out of necessity" response to a highly dangerous situation that affects us all. There may also be other, less tangible factors involved. For example, the late French paleontologist-theologian Pierre Teilhard de Chardin believed that we are undergoing a planetary evolution toward an "Omega point of awareness," which will eventually lead to the spiritual unity of humankind. In such an ideal world there would be no need for psychological barriers and military armaments.

Amid the constant daily news of inhumanities toward our fellow beings, it is heartening to hear the encouragement of those like the United Nations' Robert Muller, who believe that sanity and human decency will yet prevail. Such optimism helps give a sense of direction, purposefulness, and empowerment to those who are discouraged by the seeming endlessness of the road of peacemaking that lies ahead.

A growing number of people in all parts of the world are developing a "one-humanity" consciousness and sharing what they have learned with others. The practice of "thinking globally, acting locally," is beginning to take root. This involves working within one's own community and simultaneously being aware of the planetary implications of one's actions. A special responsibility to meet the life-threatening crisis rests in the hands of the citizenry of the superpowers, especially here in the United States, with our long-standing freedoms of speech and public assembly.

Stephen Longfellow Fiske is a minstrel whose musical evolution reflects the times in which he has lived. His songs evoke his experience of the turbulent politics of the 1960s and his quest in the 1970–1980s for a holistic approach to life. His song "Seeds of Peace," written in the 1970s, speaks for itself:

> When the wind sweeps across the plains
> bearing seeds upon its wings
> and the sun comes behind the rain
> as the winter turns to spring
> then the seeds root down in the earth
> and new sprouts are then released
> and all life celebrates the birth
> of seeds of peace
>
> We have climbed every mountaintop
> we have sailed to every shore
> we have crossed the earth with border lines
> we have lost our sons in war
> but the seeds on the open wind
> know no boundary lines of war
> they will wash the battleground with green
> and the peace shall be restored
>
> Lay me down by a mountain stream
> lay me down upon the shore
> let me feel the earth return to spring
> let me hear her song once more
> may the seeds that have brought us birth
> fill the needs that all hearts seek
> to be free to grow upon the earth
> and live in peace
>
> (Chorus)
> Know them now
> sow them now
> seeds of peace[12]

The scope and complexity of the world's problems often seem so overwhelming it is easy to forget that positive change is possible. This idea is very simply, but powerfully expressed in the words of the psalmist, "For everything there is a season, and a time for every purpose under heaven" (Ecclesiastes 3:1). Seeds for peace are being sown. They take time to germinate; but the small shoots which have pushed to the surface are evidence that the growth process has begun. These seedlings will require careful nurturance to achieve their full potential. Their very existence, though, indicates that sanity and human dignity can yet prevail.

In confronting the nuclear danger, peaceful demonstrations and appeals to conscience in any locale resonate within and beyond national and continental boundaries. Each personal effort, whether it be educating oneself and others, working with concerned groups, petitioning elected representatives, meditating, or sharing prayer, has intrinsic value.

The ancient Chinese character for "crisis" connotes both danger and opportunity. Similarly, the Bomb, which presents the danger of annihilation, also offers an unexpected opportunity for building life-giving human community. Working cooperatively to dismantle the weapons of destruction, and the fears and negativity they symbolize, may help humankind to forge the heretofore "missing link" of a sense of species-hood.

Experience gained in this shared endeavor could have many other positive spinoffs as well—making it easier to focus worldwide attention on such vital problems as providing sustenance for the hungry, securing basic human rights, and protecting the biosphere and endangered life-forms. Much needs to be done. Each person's participation, wherever she or he may be, has significance and takes us one step further towards the discovery of our common ground. Every earnest contribution, however humble it may appear, will help in the global effort to move away from the precipice of destruction and toward the enhancement of life.

Notes

1. David Spangler, "On the New Humanity," a transcribed talk at the Omega Institute's 1979 summer conference, Bennington College, Vt.

2. Robert Muller, *New Genesis: Shaping a Global Spirituality* (New York: Doubleday, 1982).

3. Lillie Wilson, "The Planetary Initiative: A Plot to Save the World," *New Age Journal* (January 1982): 42–45.

4. Darshan Singh, *Spiritual Awakening* (Bowling Green, Va.: Sawan Kirpal Publications, 1982), 7.

5. Jean Houston, "The Power of Acknowledgment," *New Age Journal* (May 1979): 38.

6. David Spangler, "The Reappearance of the Mystery Schools," *Lindisfarne Letter* (Summer 1978): 12.

7. M. Scott Peck, *The Road Less Traveled: A New Psychology of Love, Traditional Values, and Spiritual Growth* (New York: Simon and Schuster, Touchstone, 1978), 81–84.

8. June Singer, *Androgyny: Toward A New Theory of Sexuality* (New York: Doubleday, Anchor, 1976).

9. Elizabeth Dodson Gray, *Patriarchy as a Conceptual Trap* (Wellesley, Mass.: Roundtable Press, 1982).

10. Lyall Watson, *Lifetide: The Biology of the Unconscious* (New York: Bantam, 1980), 147–48.

11. Ken Keyes puts forth some suggestions on what can be done about the nuclear challenge in *The Hundredth Monkey* (St. Mary, Ky.: Vision Books, 1981).

12. Transcribed from a tape cassette, "Seeds of Peace: An Album of Songs by Stephen Longfellow Fiske," produced by the composer in 1979.

Selected Bibliography

Books

Alinsky, Saul. *Rules for Radicals*. New York: Random House, 1972.

Berry, Wendell. *The Gift of Good Land*. North Point Press, 1981.

Bohm, David. *Wholeness and the Implicate Order*. Boston: Routledge and Kegan Paul, 1980.

Boyte, Harry. *The Backyard Revolution: Understanding the New Citizen Movement*. Philadelphia: Temple University Press, 1980.

Campbell, Alastair, et al. *Worker Owners: The Mondragon Achievement*. London: Anglo-German Foundation, 1977.

Capra, Fritjof. *The Tao of Physics*. New York: Bantam, 1977.

Carr, John, and Rosemary Taylor. *Coops, Communes and Collectives: Experiments in Social Change in the 1960s and 1970s*. New York: Pantheon, 1979.

Clecak, Peter. *America's Quest for the Ideal Self: Dissent and Fulfillment in the 60s and 70s*. New York: Oxford University Press, 1983.

Coates, Gary J., ed. *Resettling America: Energy, Ecology, and Community*. Andover, Mass.: Brick House, 1981.

Cooney, Robert, and Helen Michalowski, eds. *The Power of the People: Active Non-Violence in the United States*. Culver City, Calif.: Peace Press, 1977.

Cox, Harvey. *Turning East: The Promise and Peril of the New Orientalism*. New York: Simon and Schuster, 1977.

Day, Dorothy. *Loaves and Fishes*. New York: Harper and Row, 1963.

Douglass, James W. *Lightning East to West: Jesus, Gandhi, and the Nuclear Age*. New York: Crossroad, 1983.

169

Elgin, Duane. *Voluntary Simplicity.* New York: Bantam, 1982.

Farren, Pat, ed. *What Will It Take to Prevent Nuclear War?* Cambridge: Schenckman, 1983.

Ferguson, Marilyn. *The Aquarian Conspiracy: Personal and Social Transformation in the 1980s.* Los Angeles: J. B. Tarcher, 1980.

The Food Co-op Handbook. Boston: Houghton Mifflin, 1975.

Friends Can Be Good Medicine. Sacramento: California Department of Mental Health, 1981.

Fromm, Erich. *Revolution of Hope.* New York: Harper and Row, 1968.

Gaskin, Stephen. *This Season's People.* Summertown, Tenn.: The Book Publishing Company, 1976.

Gillingham, Peter, and E. F. Schumacher. *Good Work.* New York: Harper and Row, 1980.

Gray, Elizabeth Dodson. *Patriarchy as a Conceptual Trap.* Wellesley, Mass.: Roundtable Press, 1982.

Ground Zero. *Nuclear War, What's in It for You?* New York: Pocket, 1982.

Hedgepeth, William, and Dennis Stock. *The Alternative: Communal Life in New America.* New York: Macmillan, Collier, 1970.

Kanter, Rosabeth Moss. *Commitment and Community: Communes and Utopias in Sociological Perspective.* Cambridge: Harvard University Press, 1972.

Kübler-Ross, Elisabeth. *On Death and Dying.* New York: Macmillan, 1969.

Lappe, Frances Moore. *Diet for a Small Planet.* New York: Ballantine, 1975.

Lappe, Frances Moore, and Joseph Collins. *Food First: Beyond the Myth of Scarcity.* New York: Ballantine, 1979.

Laszlo, Ervin, and Donald Keys, eds. *Disarmament: The Human Factor.* Elmsford, N.Y.: Pergamon, 1981.

Longacre, Doris Janzen. *Living More with Less.* Scottdale, Pa.: Herald Press, 1980.

Lovins, Amory B. *Soft Energy Paths: Toward a Durable Peace.* New York: Harper and Row, 1979.

McRobie, George. *Small Is Possible.* New York: Harper and Row, 1981.

Miller, William. *Dorothy Day: A Biography.* New York: Harper and Row, 1982.

Montgomery, Ruth. *Strangers among Us.* New York: Fawcett, Crest, 1982.

Moody, Philip. *Life after Life.* Tallahassee: Mockingbird Press, 1975.

Muller, Robert. *New Genesis: Shaping a Global Spirituality.* New York: Doubleday, 1982.

Nash, Hugh, ed. *Progress As If Survival Mattered: A Handbook for a Conserver Society,* 2d ed. San Francisco: Friends of the Earth, 1981.

Nearing, Scott, and Helen Nearing. *Continuing the Good Life: Half a Century of Homesteading*. New York: Schocken, 1979.

————. *Living the Good Life*. New York: Schocken, 1970.

Needleman, Jacob. *The New Religions*. New York: Doubleday, 1970.

Oates, Stephen. *Let The Trumpet Sound: The Life of Martin Luther King, Jr*. New York: Harper and Row, 1982.

Peck, M. Scott. *The Road Less Traveled: A New Psychology of Love, Traditional Values, and Spiritual Growth*. New York: Simon and Schuster, Touchstone, 1978.

Reader, Mark, ed. *Atom's Eve: Ending the Nuclear Age*. New York: McGraw-Hill, 1980.

Ring, Kenneth. *Life at Death: A Scientific Investigation of the Near-Death Experience*. New York: Coward, McCann and Geoghegan, 1980.

Robertson, Laurel, Carol Flinders, and Bronwen Godfrey. *Laurel's Kitchen: A Handbook for Vegetarian Cooking and Nutrition*. Berkeley: Nilgiri Press, 1976.

Ronco, William. *Food Coops*. Boston: Beacon Press, 1974.

Roszak, Theodore. *Person/Planet*. New York: Doubleday, Anchor, 1978.

Satin, Mark. *New Age Politics: Healing Self and Society*. New York: Delta, 1979.

Schell, Jonathan. *The Fate of the Earth*. New York: Alfred A. Knopf, 1982.

Schumacher, E. F. *Small Is Beautiful: Economics As If People Mattered*. New York: Harper and Row, 1973.

Sharp, Gene. *The Politics of Non-Violent Action*. 3 vols. Boston: Porter Sargent, Extending Horizons Books, 1980.

Singer, June. *Androgyny: Towards a New Theory of Sexuality*. New York: Doubleday, Anchor, 1976.

Singh, Darshan. *Spiritual Awakening*. Bowling Green, Va.: Sawan Kirpal Publications, 1982.

Smallwood, Frank. *The Other Candidates: Third Parties in Presidential Elections*. Hanover, N.H., and London: University Press of New England, 1983.

Thomas, Norman. *Socialism Re-examined*. New York: W. W. Norton, 1963.

VandenBroeck, G., ed. *Less Is More: The Art of Voluntary Poverty*. New York: Harper and Row, 1978.

Wasserman, Harvey. *Energy War: Reports from the Front*. Westport, Conn.: Lawrence Hill, 1979.

Watson, Lyall. *Lifetide: The Biology of the Unconscious*. New York: Bantam, 1980.

Yankelovich, Daniel. *New Rules*. New York: Random House, 1981.

Zinn, Howard. *A People's History of the United States*. New York: Harper and Row, 1980.

Articles

"Beyond Price: The Story of H.O.M.E." *Peacework,* no. 108 (May 1982): 12.

Height, Dorothy. "From Mississippi to Maseru: Women in Community Development." *Journal of Community Action: Community Development at Home and Abroad,* vol. 1, no. 6 (1983): 9–16.

Houston, Jean. "The Power of Acknowledgment." *New Age Journal* (May 1979).

Hunt-Perry, Patricia, and Arthur Stein. "Seeds of Change: A Time of Reorientation." *Phoenix: A Journal of Transpersonal Anthropology,* vol. 5, no. 1 (1981): 67–78.

Kotzsch, Ronald. "The Irrepressible Scott Nearing." *East-West Journal* (February 1981): 34–39.

Nelson, Juanita. "Bypassing the Buck." *New Roots: The Magazine of Energy, Community, and Self-Reliance* (Spring 1982): 24–27.

Sleeper, Jim. "A Toddler with Determination." *In These Times* (June 16–29, 1982).

Spangler, David. "The Reappearance of the Mystery Schools." *Lindisfarne Letter* (Summer 1978): 12.

Stein, Arthur. "Cooperatives: An Alternative Institution." *News: A Publication of the American Political Science Association,* no. 24 (Winter 1980): 1, 10–11.

———. "Scott and Helen Nearing: A Tribute." *The Sun: A Magazine J. of Ideas,* no. 104 (July 1984): 28–33.

———. "Towards Alleviating Poverty and Promoting Human Dignity in Rural America." *Gandhi Marg* (Journal of the Gandhi Peace Foundation, New Delhi), no. 42 (September 1982): 569–79.

Von Ranson, Joanathan. "Wendell Berry: A Farmer Poet Resettling America." *New Roots: The Magazine of Energy, Community, and Self-Reliance,* no. 20 (New Year, 1982): 16–20.

Wilson, Lillie. "The Planetary Initiative: A Plot to Save the World." *New Age Journal* (January 1982): 42–45.

Other specific references to articles, newsletters, resource groups, national public media, conference talks, and informational publications by political, community, and cooperative organizations can be found in the chapter notes.

Periodicals

Akwesasne Notes (Rooseveltown, N.Y.)
The Alternative newsletter (Kingston, R.I.)
Catholic Worker (New York, N.Y.)
Christian Science Monitor (Boston, Mass.)
Co-Evolution Quarterly (Sausalito, Calif.)

Common Cause (Washington, D.C.)
Communities Magazine (Louisa, Va.)
Co-op: The Harbinger of Economic Democracy (Ann Arbor, Mich.)
Dandelion (Philadelphia, Pa.)
Democratic Left (New York, N.Y.)
Directory of Intentional Communities (Louisa, Va.)
East-West Journal (Brookline, Mass.)
Fellowship (Nyack, N.Y.)
The Food Co-op Directory (Albuquerque, N. Mex.)
Friends Journal (Philadelphia, Pa.)
Gandhi Marg (New Delhi, India)
Green Revolution (York, Pa.)
Guide to Alternative Periodicals (Greenlead, Oreg.)
A Guide to Cooperative Alternatives (New Haven, Conn., and Louisa, Va.)
In These Times (Chicago, Ill.)
The Independent Man (Providence, R.I.)
Journal of Community Action (Washington, D.C.)
Maine Land Advocate (Augusta, Maine)
Manus (Los Angeles, Calif.)
Mobilization for Survival (Philadelphia, Pa.)
Moment (Boston, Mass.)
Mother Earth News (Hendersonville, N.C.)
Mother Jones magazine (Boulder, Colo.)
New Age Journal (Brighton, Mass.)
New Options (Washington, D.C.)
New Roots: The Magazine of Energy, Community, and Self-Reliance (Greenfield, Mass.)
New York Times (New York, N.Y.)
Northeast Sun (Brattleboro, Vt.)
Not Man Apart (San Francisco, Calif.)
Nuclear Times (New York, N.Y.)
Nucleus: Union of Concerned Scientists Newsletter (Cambridge: Mass.)
Peacehaven (Deer, Ark.)
Providence Journal (Providence, R.I.)
Rain magazine (Portland, Oreg.)
Renewal: New Values, New Politics (Washington, D.C.)
Rural Advocate newsletter (Charlotte, N.C.)
SANE Action: The Newsletter of the Rapid Response Network (Washington, D.C.)
Self-Reliance newsletter (Washington, D.C.)
Sharing Life (Little Rock, Ark.)
Sojourners magazine (Washington, D.C.)
Spiritual Community Guide (San Rafael, Calif.)

The Sun: A Magazine of Ideas (Chapel Hill, N.C.)

Vocations for Social Change (Boston, Mass.)

Whole Life Times (Newton, Mass.)

Win: Peace and Freedom through Non-Violent Action (Brooklyn, N.Y.)

Women for a Non-Nuclear Future newsletter (Providence, R.I.)

Working Papers for a New Society (Cambridge, Mass.)

Acknowledgments

The thought of doing a book on positive undercurrents within American society had been in the back of my mind for some time during the 1970s. But without the encouragement of two good friends, Michael Purdy and Patricia Hunt-Perry, the idea might not have come to fruition. Michael and I were coordinators of a stimulating Honors Colloquim on "Creativity and the Human Spirit" at the University of Rhode Island in 1977–78. The following year Patricia helped me develop a focus for the book and made many useful suggestions as the manuscript evolved.

Other friends and co-workers whom I wish to thank include Helen Zimmermann, Debbie Purdy, Shirley Lee, Gary and Audrey Post, Rajiv Vora, Al Killilea, and Clara Johnson. Each in his or her own way has been very supportive during my work on this project.

Some of those about whom I have written in *Seeds of the Seventies* I have known for a long time; others I have met only briefly. Many of those whom I have not had the pleasure of meeting, I nonetheless feel I know through their writings and good work. Each of these persons is helping to make the vision of a just and caring society more of a living reality.

I am indebted to a generation of URI students who have participated in courses I have offered on "Dissent, Non-Violence and Living in the Nuclear Age," "Cooperatives and Communities," "Eastern and Western Thought," and "Alternative Prospects for

Humankind." We have explored together many of the subjects discussed in this book, and I have benefitted from their creative input and occasional good-natured skepticism. I wish to give special thanks to Gretchen Test, Chris DePaola, Trish Miller, Jim Schaffer, Alan Silverman and Michael Vocino and, going back to Project '70 days, Steve and Sue Feldman, Linda Atamian, Marilou and Paul Murphy, Marty Milner, and Steve Cohen—all of whom helped to transform the college classroom into a cooperative learning community. And thanks to those who have kept the spirit of conscientious student activism alive—from Gary Ferdman in the Vietnam years to Dan Szumilo and Christin Schmidt of the current URI Students for Social Change. Also a word of appreciation to Frank and Sharon Forleo for their often unsung work on behalf of disadvantaged students in the URI Talent Development Program, and to John Hall, Joan Mahoney, Randy Chew, and the other University Chaplains who have taken the initiative in bringing Peace Studies to our community.

For their encouragement over the years, I wish to thank each of my colleagues in the URI Political Science Department. My gratitude also goes to Professors Phyllis Brown, Aloys Michel, and Shashanka Mitra, who have been most supportive of this project. I am appreciative of the cooperation extended by the editors and staff of University Press of New England, and the skillful copy-editing of Susan S. M. Brown. As "outside readers" for the UPNE Professors Robert White and Charles Hauss each provided many valuable suggestions for the improvement of the manuscript.

Parts of several chapters have appeared in somewhat different form in articles in *Gandhi Marg: The Journal of the Gandhi Peace Foundation; The Sun: A Magazine of Ideas;* and *Phoenix: Journal of Transpersonal Anthropology.* I thank the editors of these journals for permission to include some of this material.

As I am still of the pad and pencil school, I am grateful to Sharon Woodmansee, Jean Gefrich, and Delores Eaton, who exercised patience and good cheer in deciphering parts of the manuscript and rendering it into typewritten form.

Finally, my deepest love to daughters Lisa and Jody and my parents Mary and Samuel Stein, to whom this book is dedicated.

Index

Ronstadt, Linda, 111
Roszak, Theodore, 23; *Person/Planet*, 80
Rotkin, Mike, 86
Rowny, Edward, 113
Rural Advancement Fund (North Carolina), 35–37
Rural America: back-to-the-land movement, 24–32; farmworkers movement, 12, 37, 40; intentional communities, 10, 46–47, 60–66, 149; new towns concept, 38–40, 61–63; self-help projects, 32–41, 148

Salk, Hilary, 90
Sanders, Bernard, 89
Sandhill (Missouri), 60
Sant Mat, 20
Sarkady, Marc, 142
Satin, Mark, 9, 134–39; *New Age Politics*, 135
Schell, Jonathan: *The Fate of the Earth*, 107
Schlafly, Phyllis, 13
Schumacher, E. F., 50, 74–75; *Good Work*, 14, 75; *Small Is Beautiful: Economics As If People Mattered*, 14, 74–75
Science, 22
Scott-Bader Commonwealth, 80
Seabrook (New Hampshire) nuclear power plant, 117–19
Seed conservation, 37–38
Seeger, Pete, 15, 118
Self-exploration. *See* Personal growth
Self-help projects, rural, 32–41; HOME, 14, 32–34, 148; Institute for International Economics, 40; Koinonia, 34–35, 41n7; National Sharecroppers Fund, 37–38, 148; New Communities Incorporated, 39–40, 61, 148; Rural Advancement Fund, 35–37
Service to others, 128–31, 149–50; Catholic Worker, 87, 97, 128–29, 149; Committee for Creative Non-Violence, 129, 149; Highlander Folk School, 129–31
Shakertown Pledge, 127–28

Simplicity. *See* Voluntary simplicity
Singer, June, 139, 159; *Androgony*, 14
Singh, Sant Darsham, 158
Singh, Sant Kirpal, 19, 141
Sirius educational community (Massachusetts), 10
Small Farms Research Organization, 27
Smith, Bill, 76–77
Social relationships, 47, 158–59
Society of Friends, 57, 94, 143
Southern Christian Leadership Conference, 10, 98
Southern Mutual Self-Help Association, 37
Southern Tenant Farmers Union, 37
Southwest Georgia Project, 39
Spangler, David, 150, 158
Species consciousness, 152–54, 163–64
Spirituality, 17–21; and death, 22–23; Eastern, 18–20, 22; and knowledge and science, 21–22; and nonviolence, 93–94, 104; Western, 20
Spock, Benjamin, 83
Springsteen, Bruce, 111
Steinem, Gloria, 86
Stop Wasting Abandoned Property (SWAP), 69–71
Sufism, 20
Sumitra, 154
Sun Bear, 12
Suzuki, D. T., 18
Suzuki, Shaunryu, 19
Swann, Bob, 40
Swann, Marge, 102

Tarrytown Letter, The, 138, 144n8
Taylor, James, 111
Technology, alternative, 74–82, 142
Teilhard de Chardin, Pierre, 164
Teresa (Mother), 15
Terkel, Studs, 87
Thomson, Meldrim, 117
Thoreau, Henry David, 25
Todd, John and Nancy, 77
Toffler, Alvin, 59
Transformational movement, 133–44; and activism, 142–43; Human Unity Conference, 141–42; litera-